"Diana captures the essence of joyfu[l]
positive words will encourage any mi[nister's wife for]
years; she's living proof of the fulfilling ministry she writes about."

—ANN IORG, president's wife, Golden Gate Baptist Theological Seminary

"I wholeheartedly recommend *Six Simple Steps* for every minister's wife, regardless of the place of service or the length of time you have been in ministry. We are all in this together and Diana coaches us with encouraging words and a hopeful message."

—PAM LANCE, wife of executive director, Rick Lance,
Alabama Baptist State Board of Missions

"Every ministry wife needs this excellent resource on her nightstand, whether you are beginning the journey or have been at it for many years. Davis's 'six steps' are clear, succinct, and full of wisdom."

—SUSIE HAWKINS, author, women's ministry leader, ministry wife

"If you are a minister's wife, you *need* this book. Diana Davis offers boundless wisdom with tried-and-true tips for enjoying your calling. This must-read will enhance your ministry and encourage your heart as you serve alongside your husband."

—AUTUMN WALL, worship leader, Living Faith Church, Indianapolis, IN

"My dear friend provides this invaluable, relevant tool for ministry wives. Diana Davis's Spirit-led wisdom on embracing your missions field, 60-second joy boosters, and fresh ways to love the hurting whom God places in your life are some of the practical insights she shares. I read, and left encouraged to complete the plans the Lord has for us. I am excited to share this treasure with my dear sisters who serve faithfully to further the kingdom."

—LYNETTE EZELL, wife of Kevin Ezell, president of the North American Mission Board

"When you pick up Diana's book, you have met a friend!"

—KATHLEEN HARDAGE, wife of executive director, Baptist General Convention of Texas

"A practical primer for ministry wives, *Six Simple Steps* can move us from being nominal to being radical difference makers. Diana Davis lives this book. The steps are simple but oh-so powerful. Step three, "Love Lavishly," reminds us that our reckless love can make eternal difference."

—KATHY FERGUSON LITTON, national consultant for
Ministry to Pastor's Wives, flourish.me

"What a combination for women with ministry hearts! Gifted with her pen and winsome style, coupled with the awesome lens she uses to analyze and unpack timely and inspirational ideas, Davis moves from the importance of being comfortable with who you are in Christ to how you can lavish His grace on those around you. This is a must-read for women whose husbands are in ministry positions—and any woman who wants to maximize her influence in the kingdom and beyond."

—DOROTHY KELLEY PATTERSON, First Lady, and professor of theology in women's studies, Southwestern Baptist Theological Seminary, Fort Worth, TX

"If you are in the ministry one day or 41 years, this book is a precious challenge to be your best for Christ, your family, and His work. Diana has presented simple, concise, clear steps to deepen our intimate walk with Jesus. This is a 'Ministry Wife 101' course book I wish I had had when I began the 'high calling' role of being a pastor's wife in 1973! Godspeed!"

—JUNE RICHARDS, wife of Southern Baptists of Texas Convention executive director

"Every minister's wife can find something in this book to help in her work."

—WILSENE KWOK, wife of State Convention of Baptists in Ohio executive director

"Diana's love for each pastor's wife shines through. *Six Simple Steps* is full of practical advice from someone who has experienced the good and the tough times of ministry yet has come through with only love for Christ and the church. I found myself devouring every page, wishing that I had received this book as a new pastor's wife."

—SARAH BOHRER, children's ministry director, State Convention of Baptists in Indiana

"*Six Simple Steps* encourages and challenges those of us who call ourselves ministry wives. In the 44 years I have known Diana Davis, she has consistently and passionately modeled these steps. Thanks, Diana, for writing such a timely and needed book!"

—BRENDA SWOFFORD, pastor's wife, First Baptist Church, Rockwall, TX

"Diana Davis has created a practical resource and her focus is *spot on* as she considers matters close to the hearts of women who are co-laborers with their husbands in the work of Christ. This book is a *must-have* for new ministry wives as well as an encouragement to those who have been in the trenches."

—ALLISON KINION, director of women's missions and ministry, State Convention of Baptists in Indiana, and senior pastor's wife, Calvary Baptist Church, Greenfield, IN

"It is my joy to endorse Davis's book for ministry wives. Diana has extensive experience as a ministry wife who also ministers in such a caring and encouraging way to ministry wives wherever she serves. Her new book will be a blessing to all."

—PEGGIE SEAGLE, wife of Cecil Seagle, executive director,
State Convention of Baptists in Indiana

"This is a wonderful tool for all ministry wives that I wish I had had when I first started out as a young pastor's wife. This must-read—for every ministry wife who, with God's help, wants to be the best she can possibly be—depicts Davis's excitement for serving God and her desire to help other women learn by sharing these creative ideas."

—CHERYL D. HARPER, ministry wives consultant, wife of executive director,
West Virginia Convention of Southern Baptists

"What an encouraging read! As a minister's wife all we have to be is who God made us to be. We are all uniquely different and designed by an amazing God who desires to use us where He has planted us—to love husband, children, church, and most importantly Savior. Thank you, Diana, for words that free ministers' wives to be themselves!"

—JEQUITA LEE, wife of Utah-Idaho Southern Baptist Convention executive director,
and elementary art teacher

"Diana Davis is the idea lady extraordinaire. No one else can jam this much inspiration and information into a compact book. Did I mention encouragement? And comfort? And forehead-slapping insights? *Six Simple Steps* reeks hope and oozes joy. I am happily contaminated after handling it. I plan to give a copy to every pastor's wife I know."

—CONNIE CAVANAUGH, pastor's wife, speaker, and author; conniecavanaugh.com

"Diana has done it again! What a helpful and insightful book for all ministry wives. This book births new insights each time one reads it. God spoke to me through this book and revealed areas of personal growth for me. My favorite simple step is "Love Lavishly"—Diana nailed it!"

—ROBIN SMALLEY, pastor's wife, Lakota Hills Baptist, West Chester, OH

"Read your way through Diana's guidebook for ministers' wives and you'll find yourself serving God's people with the same wholehearted enthusiasm she has demonstrated throughout her marriage. As to be expected, *Six Simple Steps* is packed with practical application of biblically based insight."

—TAMMI REED LEDBETTER, writer for the *Southern Baptist TEXAN*

Diana
Davis

6 Simple Steps

Finding Contentment & Joy
as a Ministry Wife

NEW HOPE
PUBLISHERS
Gospel-Centered. Missions-Driven.

BIRMINGHAM, ALABAMA

New Hope® Publishers
PO Box 12065
Birmingham, AL 35202-2065
NewHopeDigital.com
New Hope Publishers is a division of WMU®.

Library of Congress Control Number: 2014955000

Unless otherwise indicated, all Scripture quotations are taken from the Holy Bible, New Living Translation, copyright © 1996, 2004, 2007, 2013 by Tyndale House Foundation. Used by permission of Tyndale House Publishers, Inc., Carol Stream, Illinois 60188. All rights reserved.

Scripture quotations marked TLB are taken from The Living Bible copyright © 1971. Used by permission of Tyndale House Publishers, Inc., Carol Stream, Illinois 60188. All rights reserved.

Scripture quotations marked HCSB are taken from the Holman Christian Standard Bible®, Used by Permission HCSB ©1999, 2000, 2002, 2003, 2009 Holman Bible Publishers. Holman Christian Standard Bible®, Holman CSB®, and HCSB® are federally registered trademarks of Holman Bible Publishers.

Cover Design: Michel Lê
Interior Design: Glynese Northam

ISBN-10: 1-59669-422-X
ISBN-13: 978-1-59669-422-4

N154101 • 0115 • 2.5M1

Dedication

This book is dedicated to women who serve in the unique role of ministry wife—especially Brenda Swofford, Liz Traylor, Autumn Wall, Michelle Mullenix, and Sarah Bohrer.

Keep on shining, sisters!

Contents

Acknowledgments

My sincere gratitude to Autumn Wall, Liz Traylor, Nancy Schultze, Brittany Strebeck, Maggie McGowan Davis, Kris Matheus, and Jeannine McNeil. Each of you has helped me with encouragement, edit assistance, brainstorming, or unblocking writer's block. I'm blessed to have such dear and wise friends.

My managing editor at New Hope Publishers, Joyce Dinkins, who's been a prayer champion, sound sounding board, and wise counsel. Your mastery of words helps my ordinary writings come alive. Every member of your editorial and marketing team has been a blessing to me.

And, as always, my best listener, friend, encourager, and in-house Bible consultant is my beloved husband, Steve. Thanks for encouraging me to hang in there on this book. It's a true joy to serve God alongside you as a ministry wife.

Introduction

So your husband is a minister. This book is written just for you! Whether you're a brand-new ministry wife or have worn that role for years, I'm praying God will use these words to enhance your joy and contentment.

Your husband may be a pastor, chaplain, or missionary. He may lead a denomination, a seminary class, or a Christian organization. He may be an associate pastor, church planter, or evangelist. You two may serve in a rural or urban setting, or in any country across the globe. The variety of ministries is endless, yet whatever the ministry, the privileges and needs of a minister's spouse are surprisingly similar.

Let me introduce myself. Like you, I'm a minister's wife. I grew up in Fort Worth, Texas, and met my husband, Steve, at Dallas Baptist University. I was a Christian and loved God, but hadn't planned on being married to a minister. Was I in for a great surprise!

Serving God alongside a minister is a unique assignment. After decades together, I can assure you that it remains an exciting and worthwhile life. We loved serving as pastor and pastor's wife in Texas, in a church plant, a medium-sized church, and a large church. We've seen how God can use His church, full of imperfect people, to make an impact on eternity.

With all that experience, I thought I knew a lot about being a pastor's wife. That next decade, however, as Steve served as a state denominational leader in Indiana, we worshiped in hundreds of different churches. I spent time with a wide variety of ministry wives, and was in awe at all the ways God uses them to accomplish His purposes.

Those ministry wives and others I've met across the country inspired this book. It's written as a book of ideas and encouragements for you.

I've gathered six very simple tips for you, the minister's wife, to enhance your joy and ministry. You'll notice that each step is tied to the fruit of the Spirit that God freely supplies for His followers as we give our lives fully to Him. What a gift!

Each chapter is full of personal stories, practical ideas, Scriptures, and teachings. You'll find tweet-sized quotes from a variety of ministry wives, from different places, denominations, and ministries. There's also a group study guide, for when you choose to gather some other ministry wives for a study.

We've recently moved to Pensacola, Florida, where Steve now ministers as a vice president for Southern Baptists' North American Mission Board. I meet new pastors and church planters and their wives often, and I can hardly contain myself from blurting, "Oh, you're in for an exciting life! Be encouraged."

I suggest you read this book with a pen in hand. If an idea doesn't truly fit your personality or your missions field, just "X" it. If you already use the idea, put a check by it. And if you find appealing thoughts, circle them. This is a book you'll reread multiple times, so you'll enhance its worth by marking it up.

So grab your favorite drink or snack, pull up a comfy chair, and let's talk about six simple steps for a ministry wife.

Your friend,

Diana Davis

dianadavis.org

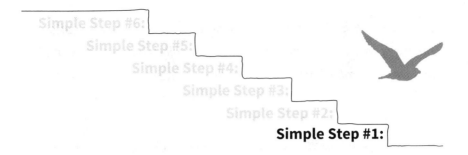

Simple Step #6:

Simple Step #5:

Simple Step #4:

Simple Step #3:

Simple Step #2:

Simple Step #1:

Just Relax

But the Holy Spirit produces this kind of fruit in our lives: . . . peace. GALATIANS 5:22

We had moved to serve in a new church and, frankly, the previous pastor's wife's reputation intimidated me. She had taught a well-attended women's Sunday School class. I liked teaching fifth-graders. She dressed meticulously. I love the casual look. She served tea in china cups. I served sandwiches on paper plates. Pretty paper plates. She'd been there 20 years. I hadn't made the 20-day mark. The first month we arrived, she was the eloquent speaker at our church's ladies retreat. My knees knocked almost audibly when I led the opening prayer. *How could I compete with all that?*

There's good news. I didn't need to compete! I simply needed to be the person God created me to be. So here's the first simple step for a ministry wife: Just relax!

"Our standard is Christ, not the pastor's wife before us or after us. God has created each unique in order to fulfill the gospel. To compare ourselves and ministry to any person steals the joy we have in Christ."

—JEN GUNN (MRS. JOEL), RALEIGH, NC

If someone who knows you well were assigned to list 100 adjectives to describe you, would the word *relaxed* be on the list? Do those around you get the impression you're frazzled or unsure of yourself? This first simple step can change that.

A ministry wife who exudes a quiet confidence is enticing. This self-confidence is not haughty. It doesn't emanate "Look at me" or "I am woman, hear me roar." It's not laziness or lack of caring. She doesn't spend her life apologizing for her inabilities. Rather, it's a God confidence that humbly conveys full trust in Him. When a ministry wife embraces God's call and direction for her life, everything changes.

God didn't create you to be a clone of the previous pastor's wife or your childhood pastor's wife or the latest "in vogue" ministry wife. It's perfectly appropriate to watch and learn from them and other Christian women you admire and respect, but don't attempt to replicate them. You are God's original, unique creation.

"No matter what anyone says, be the woman God has called you to be."

—MICHELLE MULLENIX (MRS. MONTY), BLOOMFIELD, NM

The one-of-a-kind ministry wife

Think about it. God's Word states, "I knew you before I formed you in your mother's womb" (Jeremiah 1:5). You were uniquely created to worship Him, serve Him, shine for Him. I've gathered dozens of snippets of advice from a wide variety of experienced ministry wives to share throughout this book. More than half of those tips say, essentially, "Be yourself. Your best self."

> *"You made me; you created me. Now give me the sense to follow your commands."*   PSALM 119:73

Since God intentionally created you, can you criticize His handiwork? Read this strong verse in Isaiah 29:16: *"How foolish can you be? He is the Potter, and he is certainly greater than you, the clay! Should the created thing say of the one who made it, 'He didn't make me'? Does a jar ever say, 'The potter who made me is stupid'?"*

Why complain about how God made you? God Himself gave you physical attributes, personality traits, gifts, and natural abilities different than anyone else. Thank Him, for you are "fearfully and wonderfully made" (see Psalm 139:14).

Be the one-of-a-kind woman God created, and confidently, sincerely serve Him. I love meeting ministry wives with unexpected characteristics. It boosts my awe of God to see how He can effectively use each willing vessel to accomplish His purposes.

"I'm not *like* them!" the young pastor's wife whispered. I'd invited her to a ministers' wives luncheon at our denomination's annual convention. She continued, "All those pastors' wives dress alike, and walk alike, and most have the very same *hairstyle*! I won't fit in with them, Diana." Well, I convinced her to attend, and made sure she sat at a table with a wide variety of personalities, fashionistas, and ages.

As I've spent time with many ministers' wives, a common statement I hear goes something like, "I'm not really a typical pastor's wife!" So what is a typical ministry wife? Does she teach the women's Bible class, knit, and play the piano? Does she dress frumpily and ooze sweetness? Or is she fashion-forward and nonchalant? Does she have 2.5 children and a floor clean enough to eat on? She may do all those things. *Or none of them.*

Somehow, the world—including some ministry wives—has a false impression that every ministry wife should fit some cookie-cutter mold. Don't fall for that rumor. You are one-of-a-kind.

I've known wonderful ministry wives who are tall and short, old and young, introverted and extroverted. Each has a distinct background and Christian testimony. She may wear a ponytail, pixie cut, or dreadlocks. Some wear hats or tattoos or pierced ears. I've met ministry wives who barrel race, coach, hunt, garden, trade stocks, golf, run marathons, and raise goats.

The variety in ministry wives is truly amazing. Some are factory workers, teachers, doctors, antique dealers. They are salespeople, office workers, home decorators, RNs, CPAs, CEOs, and EMTs. They may have a GED or a PhD. They're coaches, entrepreneurs, homemakers, and mechanics. They're on the city council, the PTO board, the neighborhood watch team, and the bowling league. They attend book clubs, yard sales, cattle auctions, and college classes.

They live on farms or in condos, in mobile homes, parsonages and neighborhoods. They're vegetarians, foodies, volunteers, drummers, soccer moms, readers, writers, and artists. They're childless, parents, foster parents, adoptive parents, great-grandparents. They're biscuit burners and gourmet chefs. Their individual ministries within God's church vary tremendously too. (We'll save that discussion for chap. 6.)

This list could go on, but you get the point. There *is* no cookie-cutter pattern for an effective ministry wife. Each one is uniquely created by God. As a ministry wife commits her personality, hobbies, talents, time, and resources to God, He will mold them and use them to shine for Him.

As I consider the astounding variety of God-called, one-of-a-kind women who ably, fervently, humbly serve alongside their minister-husbands, I'm truly in awe of God.

"Just be yourself. Don't try to fit into any preconceived mold of what you think a pastor's wife should look like. God made you just like you are for a reason—to bless your congregation and community in your own unique way!" —Vicki Leavell (Mrs. David), Millington, TN

Relax. God Doesn't Make Mistakes.

Have you ever felt unqualified to be a ministry wife? It's surprisingly common to hear ministers' wives voice, "I'm just not good enough" or "I'm terribly unqualified for this role" or even "I think God may have chosen the wrong woman!" Many worry incessantly about imagined or real expectations. Others wonder if God made a mistake. Some over-compensate; some balk; some commiserate. And some just trust God.

As I sat at the coffee shop with a young ministry wife, her tearful words shocked me. "I feel like a renegade pastor's wife," she blurted. "I don't care for sitting in a women's small group, but I really love leading children's church. My favorite bands are Christian rock. And I even have red hair!"

That's not renegade—she's describing her giftedness, her personality, her God-given appearance, and her uniqueness. As I've listed things about a few ministry wives I've known, I'm sure some aren't exactly like you. But renegades? Absolutely not. These women are sold out to Jesus and serving Him committedly. Distinctive? Absolutely yes! They are individual women who are called by God to serve Him alongside their husband, who happens to be a minister. Each woman has been created by God as His masterpiece. If God called your husband to be a minister, He has called you, as his wife, to serve alongside your man, using your unique personality and giftedness.

The bottom line is this: God knew. He created you. He knew exactly who you'd marry, where you'd live, and all the details that would impact your life. When God chose you to serve Him as a ministry wife,

He already knew all about your personality and gifts, your background, imperfections, quirks, and flaws. And He knew exactly how those would be used to enhance the work of ministry with your husband.

That rockin' pastor's wife? She's one of the most supportive, creative, evangelistic, committed ministry wives I know. God uses ordinary people, like you and me and that redhead, to accomplish His extraordinary purposes. So relax.

As a God follower, and as a leader, be the best you that you can be. Ephesians 4:1 challenges believers to "lead a life worthy of your calling, for you have been called by God."

"Be who God called and gifted you to be and don't get 'caught up' trying to be who a congregation wants you to be!"

—BETH ROBERTSON, VALDOSTA GA

God-Called, God-Qualified

Am I even qualified for this? There are two nonnegotiable qualifications for an effective ministry wife.

QUALIFICATION #1. YOU'RE A CHILD OF GOD.
Have you personally made a decision to be a Christian? It's the important prerequisite for an effective ministry wife! Christianity is not something we can inherit or borrow or earn. It's a personal decision. Can you name a specific time in your life when you invited God to be your personal Savior, asked His forgiveness for your sins, and committed your life to shine for Him? If you did, then you're God's child. If you're uncertain, then put down this book and find a believer—your husband or friend or me—who can help you invite God into your life. (Yes, there may be some ministry wives who are trying to live out the role, yet frustrated and confused about their eternal destiny.)

Because you've given your heart and life to God, your life purpose is to live for Him, love, and serve Him. Whether you're married to a machinist, meteorologist, or a minister, you have been chosen to serve God with your entire life. No matter what unfolds in your life, you will joyfully live for Him.

> *"I knew you before I formed you in your mother's womb. Before you were born I set you apart."*
>
> JEREMIAH 1:5

QUALIFICATION #2. YOU'RE MARRIED TO THE MINISTER.

If you are married to a minister, then you, and you alone, are the perfect ministry wife to serve alongside that man. No one else will do! God chose you, and He paired the two of you in a life-commitment marriage relationship.

The teaching in Mark 10:8, "the two are united into one," takes on important meaning. This does not imply you are the copastor. You have your own opportunities for ministry. You are his partner and supporter. You share joys. You hug him when he hurts. You love him. Of the 7 billion humans in the world, you are the one and only person who is qualified.

Not to trivialize a ministry wife's high calling, but those two qualifications are the only prerequisites. *Everything else comes out of the overflow of being God's child, who's married to a minister.* You are perfectly, uniquely qualified as a ministry wife. As you trust God with that call on your life, He will grow you and mold you and use you more than you could dream.

> *It is not that we think we are qualified to do anything on our own. Our qualification comes from God.*
>
> 2 CORINTHIANS 3:5

"For I know the plans I have for you," says the Lord. "They are plans for good and not for disaster, to give you a future and a hope." JEREMIAH 29:11

"Simply, be the person that God made you—for your husband, children, and those you are ministering to."

—TARA LAGRANGE (MRS. JOSH), FERDINAND, IN

Relaxing in the Fishbowl

As ministry wife, have you ever felt the "fishbowl effect"? It's the real or perceived feeling of someone watching your every move.

When planning a banquet for a crowd of pastors' wives in Dallas, we chose the theme No Miniblinds in the Fishbowl. The decor was extraordinary. Stringy sealike things hung from the ceilings and rose from the graveled ground. Real fish swam in bowls for centerpieces. It was all blue and green and slithery and gorgeous. It actually felt like you were standing in a fishbowl.

The finishing touch, designed by a deacon in our church, was a huge contraption sitting outside the enormous glass windows. Two three-dimensional eyeballs, complete with footlong eyelashes and a generator for an occasional blink, stared into the gigantic fishbowl.

The stage was set. That sight would terrorize every ministry wife! But the event's premise was not terror. It was about *contentment*.

When you observe an actual fishbowl, you probably notice those fish inside aren't bothered by your stares. They're happily living their fish-life—eating and swimming and playing. Fish aren't concerned about what outside observers think about their swim stroke or fin color. They don't worry about their fish identity or pedigree. They're merely busy being fish. They're content.

If you spend a lot of time fretting about observers, take a look at this

Scripture: "Watch the blameless and observe the upright" (Psalm 37:37 HCSB). New Christians are watching more mature Christians to learn how to live for God. Nonbelievers are watching to see if God truly makes a difference in your life. Yes, there are a few critics, but you don't worry about those. You're contentedly loving your God and enjoying your life.

It's OK for them to watch! Their observant eyes give us accountability, and help us to try harder to live as we should. Fishbowl living is not something we should worry about. Be content with how God created you, where He assigned you, and how He's using you.

"Litmus test of my self-identity: Am I looking at myself in view of others or in view of Jesus? Keeps me from puffing myself up as well as beating myself down!" —LAURA CHRISTOPHERSON (MRS. JEFF), TORONTO, CANADA

Rather than fretting about your qualifications, your hair, your onlookers, or your schedule, simply relax in Christ. When you're busy about God's business, without stressing, He is honored. You may be in the middle of a dozen first-graders, a hurricane, or a church business meeting, but be calm and joyful, neither haughty nor self-depreciating. God didn't make a mistake when He called you. He chose you. He's demonstrating His own greatness. Embrace your role as a ministry wife. Ministry is a lifestyle, not a job. Relax and trust God. He's got you!

NEXT STEP
TAKE ACTION
A LOOK AT THE BOOK
SIMPLE FRESH IDEAS   **NINE TIPS FOR FISHBOWL DWELLERS**

- Avoid performing. My friend, Laura says, "The church and the world have enough plastic personalities. They need to see real women who really love Jesus." Amen. Just be real.
- Remember that fish swim in schools. Don't be a Lone Ranger ministry wife.

- Fish don't drown. (At least I don't think they do!) They thrive in the water. You were created for this.
- Your home fishbowl doesn't have to be perfect to practice hospitality. Make a pathway through the kids' toys and light a candle in the bathroom.
- One ministry wife says, "When the doorbell rings, I write *Welcome* in the dust."
- Don't go for perfection. Look your best, then relax.
- Remember: if you live in a fishbowl, you'll likely get wet. Learn to enjoy it.
- Allow your fishbowl children to relax too.
- Let your fishbowl husband put his feet on the coffee table, and relax.

"Be yourself! Don't try to fit any pastor's wife 'mold.' Let God use you to be a blessing just the way you are."

—JANEY CARRICO (MRS. DAVID), PARKERSBURG, WV

NEXT STEP
TAKE ACTION
A LOOK AT THE BOOK
SIMPLE FRESH IDEAS   **HOW TO RESPOND TO GOD'S CALL**

LUKE 1:37–47

Our response to God's call should not be, "Why me, Lord?" In Luke 1:37–47, an angel has told Mary she will mother God's Son, Jesus. We can learn from how she responded to God's call. Let's look at five appropriate reactions to God's call.

Trust Him (v. 38). Say, "Yes, Lord." Mary's exact words were, "I am the Lord's servant. May everything you have said about me come true." Will you totally trust your Creator as you respond to His call on your life? He loves you and cares about every detail of your life.

Praise Him (vv. 46–47). Mary sings God's praises. She declares, "Oh, how my soul praises the Lord. How my spirit rejoices in God my Savior!" She certainly didn't understand the details of this calling. She couldn't fathom the joys and pains ahead. But she knew her God. And she knew His glory. And she praised Him. Do you hesitate or complain or stomp your foot? Or do you praise your great God for His call on your life?

Thank Him. Mary states, "For he took notice of his lowly servant girl, and from now on all generations will call me blessed. For the Mighty One is holy, and he has done great things for me." Amazing! Even in the shock of the moment, Mary shouted her thanks to God for the blessing of His call on her life.

Remember past blessings (vv. 48–55). Mary recounts the history of God's great works in her own life and throughout history. As you look back, can you see how God has prepared you for such a day as this?

Rejoice in your call (v. 47). "How my spirit rejoices in God my Savior!" Rather than fretting, Mary rejoices. Will you consistently demonstrate joy as your answer to God's call?

I want to respond like Mary. My heart's desire is to praise Him sincerely, to trust Him completely, to thank Him constantly, to never forget all His blessings, and to rejoice in His call on my life.

My favorite verse in that Luke passage states, encouragingly, "For nothing will be impossible with God" (v. 37 HCSB). I've got to admit that, even after years as a ministry wife, I am still in awe that God can use me. But I have learned to relax and trust the God of the universe.

"Relax. Breathe deeply. Trust God with every single thing."

—DEBBIE EDDINGTON (MRS. DAN), SHOREWOOD, IL

NEXT STEP
TAKE ACTION
A LOOK AT THE BOOK
SIMPLE FRESH IDEAS **MY COMMITMENT TO GOD**

❑ I will be grateful.

❑ I will relax and truly trust my God.

❑ I will praise God for His call on my life.

❑ I will be satisfied with how God created me.

❑ I will trust God completely, and relax in that trust.

❑ I will help my child be content as the minister's kid.

❑ I will try hard to be the best "me" I can be, to God's glory.

❑ I will not covet other ministry wives' spiritual gifts, talents, looks, or possessions.

NEXT STEP
TAKE ACTION
A LOOK AT THE BOOK
SIMPLE FRESH IDEAS

Pick some of these action assignments to reinforce your study about "Simple Step #1: Just Relax."

❑ Write out the story about when you became a Christian and how that impacts your everyday life. Include who, what, when, where, why, how, and tweak your words until you can read it in one minute. If you can share the basic story in a minute, you can always add details to make it longer.

❑ Share your God story aloud with someone this week.

❑ Talk with your children about God's call on their lives. Share the Bible study about Mary's response to God's call on her life, and help them be joyful in how God can use them.

❑ Try this illustrative activity. Walk outside, turn the water hose all the way on, and go to your yard's center. Let that water represent God's power. Point the nozzle straight up in the air, hold it firmly in place, and try to avoid getting wet. (You will be wet. Very wet.) Total trust in

God is like that. When we're under God's power, it's going to show all over us!

☐ Memory challenge: Make a commitment to memorize one assigned verse of Scripture for each chapter you read of this book. Today's verse: "It is not that we think we are qualified to do anything on our own. Our qualification comes from God" (2 Corinthians 3:5).

☐ Call a ministry wife you've met, who is different from you, and invite her to lunch. Listen. Learn. Pray with her.

☐ *Discuss these questions with another ministry wife:

  ■ What's your best tip for living in a fishbowl?

  ■ What's your favorite part of being married to a minister?

  ■ How are you different from other ministry wives you know?

  ■ How does God use that?

  When did you know you'd be a ministry wife?

☐ A one-week dare: Demonstrate your full trust in God this week by eliminating the phrase "I'm so busy" from your vocabulary. If you accidentally say the words, start your seven days over.

☐ Make a private list of things about yourself that might negatively impact how God can use you in ministry. These can be physical characteristics, character flaws (sin), background, personality type, and so on. Pray to commit every tidbit of your life to His glory, then put that list in the paper shredder.

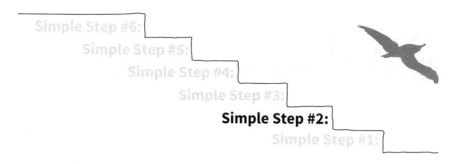

Simple Step #6:
Simple Step #5:
Simple Step #4:
Simple Step #3:
Simple Step #2:
Simple Step #1:

Simply Smile

But the Holy Spirit produces this kind of fruit in our
lives: . . . joy.   GALATIANS 5:22

The sound guy hears all. I stopped by the sound booth just after the ministry wives event. He had managed the audio system in the large group worship area, as well as some of the smaller breakout sessions rooms. I was curious to know what he thought about the meeting. "It's obvious to me," he quietly shared, "ministers' wives are some of the unhappiest women in the world."

Ouch! Do ministry wives unintentionally give the impression that being a ministry wife is miserable? Have I ever given my church members or acquaintances the impression that I'm suffering as a ministry wife? Oh, ministry and life have challenges, but God gives joy to His followers.

So our second very simple step for a ministry wife is this: simply smile. We can do that.

THE JOY VACUUM

Always be joyful. 1 THESSALONIANS 5:16

A fearsome Scripture verse is found in Moses' speech to the Israelites. As they awaited entrance to the Promised Land, Moses was explaining all the rich blessings in store if they chose to obey God there, and the curses if they chose to disobey. Joy was a part of God's instructions. Deuteronomy 28:47 states they would be punished "because if you do not serve the LORD your God with joy and enthusiasm for the abundant benefits you have received."

Shocking! Reread the reason for their potential punishment! They were serving God, but *joyful* service was what God expected. Punishment would result if they didn't serve Him with joy and a cheerful heart. How many times have we served with a passive heart, doing what was expected or promised? How much more beneficial is any small deed done with the visible joy of the Lord? Merely doing the work is not enough. God's Word instructs us to serve Him with joy.

Joy is a rare commodity in today's world, yet for God followers, joy is commanded. There is a lot to be said about joy in the Bible. The word *joy* is mentioned at least 333 times, and if you include words like *happy, glad, cheer,* and *delight,* it's more than 500 mentions.

How often should we be joyful? "This is the day the LORD has made. We will rejoice and be glad in it" (Psalm 118:24). Hmmm . . . God made *every* day. We've already discussed 1 Thessalonians 5:16's command to be joyful always. "Always" pretty much covers every minute of every day. It covers good days and bad days. A look at Paul's life reveals major problems—hunger, thirst, cold, inadequate clothing, sleepless days, snakebite, shipwreck, near death, stonings, beatings, and jail.

Yet Paul was content, and his life exuded the joy of the Lord too.

How *much* joy should a ministry wife exhibit? The Bible says we are to have abundant joy (John 16:24) and glorious, inexpressible joy (1 Peter 1:8). We are to be radiant with joy (Psalm 34:5), filled with joy (Psalm 70:4), and have overflowing joy (2 Corinthians 8:2). We are instructed to serve with joy, worship Him with joy, sing with joy, shout for joy, pray with joy. We should spill out Christian joy over whoever is near. That's a lot of joy.

Last, where does a Christian's joy come from? Galatians 5:22 teaches that the Holy Spirit Himself produces joy in a Christian's life.

You're a child of God, so smile. His Holy Spirit is filling you with joy.

The Joy Mandate

> *But let the godly rejoice. Let them be glad in God's presence. Let them be filled with joy.* PSALM 68:3

When a ministry wife lives a life of joy in Jesus, she influences others around her. Joy is contagious. As I've worshipped in many churches, I've often observed that a pastor's wife helps set the pace for joy—or lack of joy—in the church. Will you take God's instruction to be joyful as a serious assignment? Choose to be joyful. It may not always be the easiest choice, but it's always the right choice. Influence others with your consistent, joyful attitude.

When your children see you serving God with joy and living life with joy, they want more of God in their lives. As your neighbors, employer, friends, and co-workers see your joy, they will want to discover who gives that joy. Your joy will impact the atmosphere of your home and your church and your missions field. Joy trumps. Choose joy.

C. S. Lewis said, "Joy is the serious business of heaven."

Lost people can go to work, school, or anywhere else to find bickering, complaining, and misery. When they walk inside our churches, they should experience joy. They need to see joy on the faces of Christians singing about God and worshipping Him. When they are involved with your Christian organization or ministry, they observe joy. When they meet you for coffee or come to your home for fellowship, they feel the joy. When they encounter any Christian, they see joy.

"Laugh often." —CHARISSA PERRY (MRS. TOBIN), SEATTLE, WA

VISIBLE JOY

If there's joy on the inside, it needs to show on the outside. Oliver Wendell Holmes Jr., longtime US Supreme Court justice, said, "I might have entered the ministry if certain clergymen I knew had not looked and acted so much like undertakers."

I distinctly remember sitting in church by a brand-new Christian. She sang with conviction and heartfelt praise. After worship, she turned to me and asked, "How do these people sing to God with no feeling?" Even if you've been a Christian for years—*especially* if you've been a Christian for years!—demonstrate joyful praise as you worship. Rote words won't do for our great God. Casual listening isn't good enough for the sermon.

Does your hair stylist notice your joy? How about your neighbors? Your mail carrier? This admonition fits every Christian, but as a leader, you set the pace. Let your Christian joy be consistently noticeable.

JOY ON MY FACE

In my book *Deacon Wives*, I told about a neighbor who was a new Christian. Janet lived across the street from me and often came over to chat about her newfound faith. One day we were sitting in the backyard watching the kids play, and she had asked about the role of deacons in our church. She didn't know most of them, but stated confidently that she knew how to tell which women were the deacons' wives. "They're the ones with a scowl on their face!" She laughed. I scowled.

Actually I was quite offended. Our church had an amazing group of godly, loving deacons' wives. But as I thought about the ones Janet knew, those individuals actually *did* wear a scowl on their faces. Their inward joy was masked by their facial expressions.

> *A joyful heart makes a face cheerful.*
>
> PROVERBS 15:13 (HCSB)

Learn the power of a smile. The Lord fills you with joy on the inside. Let it seep out into your countenance. A grouchy face certainly doesn't mirror the joy of the Lord. A pleasant demeanor does.

Let it show. Let it show. Let it show. A sincere smile costs you nothing. It improves your appearance, enhances your approachability, lifts your attitude. You look younger and prettier. Everyone around you is impacted—your husband; children; people in your church; neighborhood; workplace. Even strangers.

Serving God is serious business, but a long-faced servant doesn't reflect well on her Master. Joy looks good on you. Smile.

"Joyfully serve the Lord alongside your husband."

—RHONDA H. KELLEY (MRS. CHUCK), PhD, NEW ORLEANS, LA

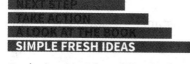

SIMPLE FRESH IDEAS   **60-SECOND JOY BOOSTERS**

Each tiny joy idea will take less than a minute. Try one this week.

- ■ This Sunday, kneel down and have a 30-second conversation with a child at church.

- Smile each time your husband walks into the room this week. (He'll think something's up!)
- Think of someone who's been an encouragement in your Christian life for many years. Call and say thanks.
- Timer test: Set a timer for one minute. Quickly comb Philippians to find a great verse about joy. Highlight it, share it, memorize it.
- Offer a sincere compliment and a smile to a teenager.
- This Sunday, walk past the newborn nursery, the church media library, and the senior adult Bible study room. Speak and smile.
- As you arrive at church, try to greet the front door greeter before he or she greets you.
- Give your minister-husband the gift of joy. Take one minute today to tell him you find great joy serving God together with him.

JOY IN MY ATTITUDE

> *A cheerful heart is good medicine, but a broken spirit saps a person's strength.*   Proverbs 17:22

I was a young newlywed attending my first meeting for ministry wives, and I was *so* excited. Miraculously, I arrived early. As I bounced up the stairs, a middle-aged woman greeted me with a stern look. "You must be a new pastor's wife," she glared. I stood there, aghast. She rolled her eyes, and said, "Don't worry, honey. You'll get over it."

I've been a ministry wife for decades now, and I still haven't "gotten over it." Being a ministry wife is not something to overcome or endure. Wherever you serve, whatever your circumstance, display a joyful attitude. Consider these two Wednesday evening scenarios:

Scene A: You rush into the church building a few minutes late again. You're exhausted and stressed and wish you were home instead.

You whisper to your husband, "You owe me," cross your arms, and grudgingly settle into the back row.

Scene B: You arrive at God's house after a full, busy day, but you're energized by the anticipation of seeing His people and being in His house tonight. Your demeanor is pleasant. Your face holds a genuine, heartfelt smile.

Both scenes feature a busy ministry wife with real-life schedules and stresses. The difference is joy. Your joy helps to create a joyful atmosphere at God's house.

Shine

This is my Seuss-like reminder, precious ministry wife, to shine with joy for Jesus. Your contentment and joy truly radiate in this dark world. Simply smile.

Shine. Shine for Jesus. Radiate. Reignite!
It's your purpose in life. Show your joy. Spread the Light.

It's the job of a wind chime to ding-a-ling-ding.
It's the job of a diamond to sparkle and bling.
It's the job of all Christians to shine for their King—
Their contentment and joy is an enticing thing.

That means Christians who are poor, and those who wear Dior.
The tweeter, the teacher, the wife of the preacher.
A teeny-bopper. Belly flopper
Kitchen mopper. Savvy shopper.
A rocket scientist, paleontologist, or domestic engineer
A doctor or an inmate or a grocery store cashier,

Laura Bush, Joe the Plumber or Sadie from Shawnee,
The CEO or BFF or L-M-N-O-P . . .

If you're a child of the Father, a child of the King,
He's given you joy and a reason to sing.
When God's living in you, then He'll shine through your life,
And the world all around you, so burdened with strife,
Will be drawn to that Light. They'll see Jesus in you.
You'll shine in the darkness. They'll notice it, too.

So in your workaday world, in your daily routine,
In the hustle or boredom or times in between…
Shine. Shine for Jesus.
Radiate. Reignite!
It's your purpose in life.
Show your joy. Spread the Light!

JOY IN MY WORDS

I was dining at an outdoor restaurant with my friend, Patty, a ministry wife. Two tourists walking past on the sidewalk stopped suddenly, then ran to our table. They were church members where Patty's husband had pastored many years ago. In the next few minutes, they repeatedly proclaimed Patty to be undoubtedly the very best pastor's wife in world's history.

Finally, I asked, "What made her the best pastor's wife in the world?" Both responded eagerly. "She always told us she *loved* being a pastor's wife!"

Patty didn't lord it over people or complain about the extra responsibilities. Instead, she simply expressed joy. Have you ever said those words aloud? "I love being a ministry wife!"

While that comment may not sound significant, it had long-lasting impact on those parishioners. Instead of playing the martyred pastor's wife, Patty had chosen joy. Don't fall into the pit of complaining. Remember: God has chosen you for this assignment. Trust Him fully, and live with joy.

A ministry wife should guard her lips. Even a slightly negative comment or complaint will appear larger to some hearers. Brag on God instead of complaining. Speak positively. Every word. Offer a sincere compliment. Express joy as you see a friend or guest. Never complain about your husband's work to your children or friends. Determine to speak your words from a joyful heart.

JOY IN MY LIFE

It's OK to have fun in ministry. Though ministry is hard work, living for Him is truly joyful. Hang out with people whose lives are characterized by Christian joy. Have fun with your husband as you serve God purposefully together. Laugh together. Enjoy today's treasures. Have fun with your children as you live out Jesus' joy. Have fun with your co-laborers in ministry and treasure the privilege of serving God with others.

I admit it. I really despise the old saying, "If Mama ain't happy, ain't nobody happy." It's unfair to put undue pressure on the woman of the house. I also must admit, however, that it's often true. When my attitude is stinky, my entire family suffers. But when I am joyful, it oozes into the attitude of every family member.

Live with joy in every circumstance. When we married, Steve was beginning seminary, and I went to work instead of completing college. I took a few more classes after he completed his degree, but as our children were born, that became my joyful priority. Once they were in high school, I went back and finished the degree, then ten years later completed a seminary degree. That was God's perfect plan for education in my life, and there was great joy in its timing and accomplishment.

Joy defines our lives and our ministry. During recent years, email and Facebook have made it easy to reconnect with friends from previous churches where we've served. Those renewed conversations often begin something like this: "Didn't we have a blast?" Yes, we worked hard. Yes, we dealt with difficulties as we planted churches and grew churches. But every day was filled with joy, and we truly had fun with those friends as we lived life together, worshipping and serving God.

I wonder if heaven might involve recounting joys. I've known many former or retired ministers' wives who recount what joy they experienced as a ministry wife. Often they hadn't thought about it until they retired. Realize you're having fun while you're having it.

> *But let all who take refuge in you rejoice; let them sing joyful praises forever. Spread your protection over them, that all who love your name may be filled with joy.* PSALM 5:11

Evangelist Billy Sunday is known to have said, "The trouble with many people is that they've got just enough religion to make them miserable. If there is not joy in religion, you have got a leak in your religion." Don't have a leak in your religion. Your joy—or lack of joy—reflects your trust in God. Decide today to live a joyful life, and say the words out loud—"I enjoy being a ministry wife."

Memory Makers

Try a few of these memory makers. Some are my ideas; others I've learned from other ministry wives. These can remind you of God's blessings and leave a legacy of joyful ministry memories for your children.

■ Begin a "blessings" journal, where you simply list God's blessings in ministry as they occur.

- Begin a notebook with tabs to list baptisms, marriages, and funerals. Even if you've been in ministry for years, begin now. You won't regret it.
- Take your husband's photo at his desk at work.
- Take a photo of your staff families or volunteer leadership team each year. If you have an annual event, take it then.
- Begin a photo book with tabs for baptisms and marriages. One ministry wife asks each couple to send her a photo of the bride and groom with the pastor.
- Ask the bride and groom to send you an update note every five years of their marriage to let you know how God is working.
- Keep a journal listing the date and name and a comment about each person with whom you or your husband have shared God's plan of salvation. If they didn't accept Christ, star their name to remind you to continue praying. A committed Sunday School teacher in our church did this privately for years, and it was quite a legacy.
- Create a memory book of church bulletins, newsletters, or special programs.
- Write in old church pictorial directories. Make notes about people and how they impacted your life. Decades from now, you may not recall some important facts.

I close my letter with these last words: Be joyful.

2 CORINTHIANS 13:11

NEXT STEP
TAKE ACTION
A LOOK AT THE BOOK
SIMPLE FRESH IDEAS   **MY COMMITMENT TO GOD**

- ❏ I will do the serious work of heaven: I will share God's joy!
- ❏ I will check my demeanor more often than I check my hair or lipstick.
- ❏ I will freely share a smile at church this Sunday.

❏ I will seriously consider 2 Corinthians 8:12 and have overflowing joy.

❏ I will tell someone in my church or ministry I love serving with them.

❏ I will have fun serving God with my husband and fellow Christians.

❏ I will laugh out loud at least once today.

❏ I will try to bring joy every time I enter a room.

NEXT STEP

TAKE ACTION

A LOOK AT THE BOOK

SIMPLE FRESH IDEAS

Pick some action activities to reinforce "Simple Step #2: Simply Smile."

❏ Do a Bible word study on *joy*.

❏ *Answer this question truthfully: What things about being a ministry wife bring you the most joy?

❏ Use your fingers to count ten people as you smile at them every day this week. If you have trouble remembering to wear a pleasant demeanor, buy some smiley-face stickers. Put them in strategic places that will annoy and remind you to show joy on your face—on your phone, computer, rearview mirror, etc.

❏ Another smile reminder idea: Ask your children or husband to help you remember to smile this week. They'll be glad to do that.

❏ Talk with your minister-husband about your peace and joy in serving God with him as a ministry wife.

❏ Choose one of the memory-maker ideas on page 36, and get started.

❏ If you have kids, use the "Shine" poem in this chapter to perform a choreographed rap. Rehearse and perform it for your husband when he comes home tonight.

❏ Buy a pretty journal today. Before sleeping tonight, write one paragraph about the blessings of being a ministry wife, and date it with month and year. Continue to write one paragraph every month this year about specific blessings related to that role.

❑ Do something unexpected, simply to spread joy. For example: Write, *God's loves you!* and put it in an envelope with some cash. Any amount you can spare is fine—$5, $20, $50. Carry the envelope in your handbag, and watch for God's prompting to give it to someone who might need or enjoy it. Give it with pure joy.

❑ Memory Challenge: "A cheerful heart is good medicine, but a broken spirit saps a person's strength" (Proverbs 17:22).

❑ Think of someone in your church or ministry who shows God's joy consistently. Take her out for a soda and learn her secrets.

❑ A weeklong challenge: Attempt to live seven consecutive days without one single whine, pout, or complaint. If you forget, start over. Make joy a new habit.

❑ *Explore these questions with another ministry wife:

- How long have you been a ministry wife?
- Have you ever told anyone that you like being a ministry wife? Why or why not?
- What brings you great joy about being a ministry wife?
- How do you make tangible memories about serving with your minister-husband?

Conversation Tips to Enhance Your Friendly Factor

- Make eye contact when you speak to people.
- Smile freely.
- Shake a hand, pat a back, touch an arm, hug a neck.
- Don't wait for others to be friendly to you. Initiate.
- Move around. Interact with as many people as possible, especially on Sunday mornings.
- Learn the art of meaningful small talk. Offer a sincere compliment. Make a kind observation.
- Ask a question. Ask an opinion. Find something you have in common.

■ If you've met the person before, call them by name. If you've forgotten it, politely ask.

■ Listen intently. Observe well. Discover needs. Converse, but don't do all the talking.

■ Give your full attention to the person speaking. Don't look at others behind them.

■ Pay particular attention to people who are alone.

■ Learn to gently delay a long conversation when you need to visit with a large group. Ask the person to sit by you, phone you, or wait just a few minutes until the crowd is gone.

■ Don't see a group or a crowd. See individuals—children, elderly, single adults, peripheral people, introverts and extroverts, leaders and nonleaders, lonely and families, rich and poor, people who sit in the back row.

Just do it! Understand the importance of being friendly. As you intentionally seek, speak, and lovingly connect with others, your ministry effectiveness rises exponentially.

Benefits of Pew-Hopping

(I said pew-hopping; not pew-jumping!)

Granted, this idea may not work for you at all, especially if you sing in the praise team or have small children. As a pastor's wife, I didn't claim any pew as mine. Instead, I chose to sit in a completely different place in the church for every worship service. It accomplished several purposes:

■ It kept my pastor-husband guessing (kidding!). He did have to glance around the balcony or back row or youth section to find where I was sitting, though.

- It helped me to know a variety of church members. I've met senior adults, children, a homeless woman, and many others I may have missed if I'd had my own "reserved" seat.

- It helped me to keep aware of guests. As I enter the worship center, I visit with various church members. At the same time, I glance around to see if there's a guest or a woman sitting alone. Then I'll sit near them.

- It allowed ministry opportunities. If I knew someone who'd had a tragedy that week, or someone with a special blessing or need, I'd find them and sit with them. I'd decide to sit with each deacon's wife over time. It was always a blessing to me.

- It helped with loneliness. A pastor's wife usually doesn't get to sit with her husband in church. Instead of pitifully sitting in a corner by yourself, look around and find someone you'd like to know better.

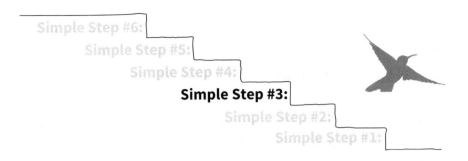

Simple Step #6:
Simple Step #5:
Simple Step #4:
Simple Step #3:
Simple Step #2:
Simple Step #1:

Love Lavishly

But the Holy Spirit produces this kind of fruit in our
lives: . . . love.　　　　　　　　　　GALATIANS 5:22

Simple step #3 for ministry wives is almost too simple. Love . . . lavishly! Your life is all about love. You're already doing it well. This chapter is simply a love refresher, challenging you to renew your love for God, your husband, your co-laborers in ministry, and your missions field. And to love them lavishly.

Love God Lavishly

You must love the LORD your God with all your heart,
all your soul, and all your strength. DEUTERONOMY 6:5

Now, that Scripture describes lavish love. Fall madly in love with your God. Our love for family, church, chocolate, and everything else in life is in a totally separate category from our love for God. He is the overarching love of our life. He alone is our single, highest focus. Ministry is not about the minister's wife. It's not about the ministry couple. It's not about church. It's all about God.

Reflect back on the day you asked God to be your Savior. That day changed your life for eternity. Your salvation was not earned because you were such a wonderful person, or because you were going to serve alongside a minister someday. God loved you before you were ever born. His love is so great that He sacrificed His only Son to pay for your sins. As you asked His forgiveness for sin, He completely forgave and became your Savior. Salvation not only provided eternal life in heaven with Him, but now you have God Himself living in you.

Here's the point: We want to love our great God with every ounce of our being. How can we do that?

STAY IN HIS PRESENCE

We stay in His presence by praying without ceasing, not just at meals and bedtime. That position changes our actions, attitudes, choices, and joy. It puts God at the center of everything. The psalmist calls it "the joy of your presence and the pleasures of living with you forever" (Psalm 16:11). When you're in His presence, you can handle anything!

READ HIS LOVE LETTERS AGAIN

It's amazing how the Bible—God's love letters to you—will continue to speak into your life. No matter how long you've been a Christian, continue to soak up His Word. It's important that a ministry wife knows how to dig into the Bible herself. Every ministry wife needs a good Bible concordance, Bible dictionary, Bible commentary, and study Bible. (Right now, I'm enjoying *The Study Bible for Women*.) Learn to use them as you relish God's love letters.

As I was working on the manuscript for this book, it was hard not to fill every page with appropriate Scriptures. At one point, I considered asking my editor if we could just print a beautiful book cover titled

Everything You Need to Know as a Ministry Wife, and then print the Bible inside! Every answer a ministry wife will ever need is right there, waiting for us. The wisest thing any ministry wife can do is to read His book.

GIVE HIM FIRST PLACE

People all around you love to advise you about your priorities. There's only one correct priority. It's God. He's not just our top priority. Every single thing in life revolves around Him.

When God is our first love, we tithe to His church faithfully and with excitement. We give offerings above the tithe, and watch for other ways to be generous to honor Him. It's quite possible you'll always serve in a church with budget needs and a building and missions program. Lead the way in supporting God's purposes financially. When God is our first love, our goals line up with His goals. We aren't "playing church" as a vocation or habit. We're loving God passionately.

TRUST HIM FULLY

You know God cares for you, and He can handle your troubles or fears. He's done it before. You trust Him with your small and huge problems, your money, family, church, chores, schedule. When your life feels inundated with blessings, you trust Him. When trials and troubles come, you trust Him. When you don't understand what's going on in your life, you trust Him. You trust Him every minute, every hour of life. Because of that trust, your love for God is lavish.

Love God

A TWO-HOUR CHALLENGE

Find a private place, such as a quiet park. Turn off your phone ringer and spend two entire hours, just you and God. Use a timer, follow this format, relax, and enjoy.

Take these supplies: iPod or CD player with Christian music, paper, a journal, pen, Bible, devotional book. Optional: a timer, your guitar (if you play).

10 Minutes	Worship	Listen to Christian music, write a poem, sketch.
20 Minutes	Pray	Use a church directory, ministry membership list, staff list, etc.
10 Minutes	Listen	Ask God to speak
10 Minutes	Journal	What He says
15 Minutes	Read Bible	An entire book
10 Minutes	Listen	And Journal
10 Minutes	Scripture	Memorize one verse
10 Minutes	Goal Setting	Ask God's direction for you
10 Minutes	Read	Devotional book
10 Minutes	Worship	Thank Him
5 Minutes	Pray	Ask God to use you

For to me, living means living for Christ.

PHILIPPIANS 1:21

Love Your Husband Lavishly

It is not good for the man to be alone. I will make a helper who is just right for him. GENESIS 2:18

Let's get personal. Your marriage relationship matters. It matters to you. It matters to your church. It matters to God. In chapter 4, we'll discuss the "we" in serving God as a married couple. But now let's talk about loving your man. Whether you've been married seven weeks or 70 years is there still a spark between you? Are you head-over-heels in love with him?

Your church and children and community observe your love for your husband. They see it in your body language, your reaction to your husband, your facial expressions. Any married couple has times they disagree, but it's strategic that a leader's marital tiffs aren't aired publicly. Truly enjoy your mate. And try a few of these ideas to remind him of your love.

TELL HIM YOU'RE HAPPY

I was chatting with a few young pastors and threw out this question: "What would be the nicest thing your wife could do for you?" One answer stabbed me in the heart! "It would be great if I could just know she's happy."

Tell him often how much you love being his wife. In conversation over dinner tonight, tell him something you love about serving in ministry with him. (Do not add a *but* to the end of the sentence.) Let him know you're very content and happy.

Our observations or ideas for improvement for the church or home can often be perceived as unhappiness to our husbands. Assure that he knows you are one happy woman.

LET HIM KNOW HE'S IMPORTANT TO YOU

Enjoy your relatives, friends, and children, but always be sure your husband knows he's first place in your relationships. Don't forget to enjoy being with him. Laugh with him often. Do small things that make him happy. Ride in the golf cart. Compliment his grilling skills. Watch his favorite movie again. If I bring my husband a candy bar, he's a happy man. Small price. Big smile.

"Second only to your personal relationship with God, your first ministry priority is your husband. He leans on God for guidance and you for support, in every area of human need." — DEBI FEHRMAN, FISHERS, IN

SAY THE WORDS

Say the words. Not just as you hang up the phone or leave the house. Look deep into your husband's eyes today, and remind him sincerely how much you genuinely love him. Let the kids hear you express your love often. Kiss him happily before he leaves and when he arrives at home. If he goes to church hours before you on Sunday, share a quick breakfast, kiss him good-bye, and hop back in bed for a few more minutes.

Here's a great idea. Purchase matching journals, and put one on his bedside table and one on yours. This is your ten-year love-letter book. Anytime you or your husband are inspired, write a short note in your spouse's book. It might be about a fun day you enjoyed together or a thank-you note. It could be an encouragement or compliment or love note. It might simply state "You're wonderful" or "I would hate to live without you." The timing is random—it might be weeks or months between notes. They don't have to be "even" in their length or frequency. You could write more notes than him, and that's fine. Read the notes to one another on your wedding anniversary.

"Be encouraging to your husband, especially when he doesn't deserve it."
—ANONYMOUS MINISTRY WIFE

BE AN UNDERSTANDING WIFE

This is a great secret to longevity in ministry as a couple. When he's down, do your very best to be up. You know and understand your husband like no one in the world. Be his refuge, a calming influence in difficult times. Be his sounding board when needed. His trusted confidante. His comfort. Listen without advising or judging. Be his constant encourager.

Be very aware of the huge responsibilities he carries and the extreme emotional drain of his work. Some days he may feel he carries the load of the world on his shoulders. His is a unique work, one that is never finished. There's always a sermon to prepare, a crisis to bear, a soul to save, or someone to help. He's always on call to minister in people's most difficult circumstances.

Help him to plan a weekly Sabbath day for rest. Try to help with his load, not to add to it. Don't try to be more important than God. Settle joyfully for second place in his life. View ministry as a marriage enhancer, not as a competition.

"Remember that your husband is a minister 24/7. He's going to need lots of prayer and you're going to need lots of patience. Keep lifting him up!" —DORA NEIGHBORS (MRS. AUTRY), ASHEVILLE, NC

MAKE YOUR HOME A HAVEN

Work hard to make your home a comforting, welcoming refuge for your husband and children. Not a fortress. Not a palace. Not a monastery. But a wonderful place of rest. Let there be a sigh of relief when he walks into the house. Allow him some relaxation moments before you hit him with today's problems.

Be content and live within your income. Honor God with how you budget your income. When a ministry couple spends more money than their income, debt can quickly distract them from God's purpose. You really can survive without a big-screen television, if necessary. I love Paul's words about how God supplies every need.

> *Not that I was ever in need, for I have learned how to be content with whatever I have. I know how to live on almost nothing or with everything. I have learned the secret of living in every situation, whether it is with a full stomach or empty, with plenty or little. For I can do everything with the help of Christ, who gives me strength. . . . And this same God who takes*

care of me will supply all your needs from his glorious riches, which have been given to us in Christ Jesus. PHILIPPIANS 4:11–13, 19

APPRECIATE HIM

Say thank you often. Thank him for working hard to provide for your family. Thank him for being a man of integrity.

I sat in a seminary's coffee shop recently, observing several ministry couples. A young man walked, smiling, across the room and delivered a couple of napkins to his wife. She glanced up with a pouty face, and growled, "I needed *three*." Her loud statement conveyed a demeaning, haughty attitude of entitlement and bossiness. She didn't appreciate his attempt at thoughtfulness. She didn't express appreciation or love. Be sure this isn't you!

PRAY FOR HIM

Be your husband's biggest prayer warrior. Remind him often that you pray for him. Pray when he preaches. Pray during business meetings. Pray when he's studying. Pray when he's handling crisis or criticism. When he's sleeping, when he's playing ball, when he's ministering in hard situations. Pray faithfully. Also, ask your husband to pray for you before you leave for work in the morning or before you go to sleep.

"Pray, pray, and pray some more for your husband. You can't be mad, angry, or disappointed when you're praying earnestly for him."
—Dottie Bass (Mrs. Steve), Phoenix, AZ

ACCEPT HIM

I once heard a pastor's wife exclaim, "He can't seem to pick up his socks. And he's a pastor!" I hate to break it to her, but being a pastor doesn't have a lot to do with socks. Remember: you picked him. This was not an arranged marriage! Accept his small faults, and love him anyway—just like he accepts yours and loves you anyway.

Never compare his physique, his golf handicap, or his sermons with another man. Accept him as God created him. Know his strong points and admire them. Know his weak points and help him. Remind him often how important he is to you.

Jesus told us to forgive one another as He forgave us. Practice forgiveness in your marriage. Forgive quickly and completely.

Each year, our church celebrated couples who'd been married 50 years. When asked her secret for marriage longevity, one wife replied, "When we first got married, my mother advised me to overlook ten of his faults for our marriage's sake. It worked!" When asked which ten faults she overlooked, she said, "Well, I never actually made the list. Each time I'd be irritated with him, I'd think, *I'll overlook that for the sake of our marriage*, and I never seemed to list ten."

ADMIRE HIM AS A MAN

Fall in love with your husband again every day. When you wake up each morning, look at him while he's sleeping and remember how much you love him. Thank God for him.

Love him physically. Remind your husband often that you find him attractive. Tell him the physical attributes and the personality traits you adore. Give him a reason to take pleasure in his wife! Dress to please him. Catch his eye across a room. Enjoy him. Remind him you love being married to him. First Corinthians 7:3 states that the husband should fulfill his wife's sexual needs, and the wife should fulfill her husband's needs. Entice him. Adore him. Romance him. Look forward to intimate time together.

Here's a tradition you might enjoy. We call it the elevator rule. Every time you happen to be riding alone in an elevator with your husband, make it a rule to give him a great big kiss. We lived on our condo's second floor in downtown Indianapolis, so the elevator rule happened often during those years. Snatch fun moments together with your husband.

Love him like a newlywed. Thelma and Wes were the oldest couple in our church plant. We couldn't have handpicked a better pair to model a loving marriage to all our young adults. They held hands. She served him tea, and called him Punkin. He doted on her every word and move, and called her Sweetie-pie. They behaved more like newlyweds than like an elderly couple married more than seven decades. Nobody who met Wes and Thelma had a doubt they were in love.

BE A FAITHFUL WIFE

Infidelity could ruin not only your marriage, but your ministry together. Don't give a hint of indiscretion or try to make your husband jealous. Be careful of your social media connections. Never show interest in any other man, even in a teasing way. If you begin to feel an attraction for another man, remove yourself from the relationship, and talk to your husband for accountability. Flirtation is a deadly game, so guard your heart. Remind your husband he's the only guy in the world for you.

First Timothy 3:2 instructs a pastor to be above reproach and faithful to his wife, and God expects no less of you. Anyone who's seen the destruction the devil can cause with infidelity in the pastor's home knows it's something to be avoided. Don't undo all you've worked for in ministry for something so trivial.

RESPECT HIM

The wife must respect her husband. EPHESIANS 5:33

We can already spell it—R-E-S-P-E-C-T—but how can we accomplish God's adamant command to respect our husband? This is especially critical for a ministry wife. Your respect for your husband influences how others view him and follow his leadership.

Here's a pop test for you. Call a close friend who knows you well. Ask this exact question: "On a scale of 1 to 10, how much would you say I respect my husband?" Listen carefully to her response. Make notes. If she says, "10," keep doing what you're doing. You are honoring God and loving your husband lavishly. If her answer is any number besides 10, improve your score.

You can say love words and do love actions, but without respect—a score of 10 on a 10-scale—there is no lavish love.

ENCOURAGE HIM

When dozens of congregants compliment the pastor's sermon, it doesn't mean nearly as much as a thumbs up from his wife. Your words of encouragement are huge. Give them freely.

"Be your husband's best supporter and encourager, his strongest prayer warrior, and his earthly 'safe place' to find love and acceptance."
—KATHY JENKINS, PLAINFIELD, IN

Love Your Co-laborers

Love each other with genuine affection, and take delight in honoring each other. ROMANS 12:10

There's a reason Scripture repeatedly commands believers to "love one another." Love shines! Think about it. Competition, apathy, backbiting, and gossip totally dismantle a church's purpose. When relationships among leaders are strained, ministry is stymied. Leaders lead by loving one another.

Do you truly and intentionally love your co-laborers in ministry? Your relationship with leaders in the church is an indispensable key to effective church ministry. If you've slipped into apathy, or even hate, it's time to reexamine those relationships. If it's your desire for God to use you and your church for His glory, love your co-laborers. Lavishly.

"I once read that church isn't a resort for the healthy but a hospital for the sick. Remembering this has helped me extend grace and mercy during painful conflicts—especially to other church staff co-laborers."

—GLENDA CHUNG (MRS. FRANCIS), LOS ANGELES, CA

A ministry wife can make an enormous difference in this area. The church mirrors its leadership. When a ministry wife loves her co-laborers, it inspires others to demonstrate that same love. Let's make a plan.

A 3-STEP PLAN TO INTENTIONALLY SHOW LOVE TO CO-LABORERS

STEP 1: THE LIST
First, make a list of important female co-laborers in ministry. For a pastor's wife, it might include vocational and volunteer ministry staff members or wives, deacon wives, the women's ministry leader, a respected women's Bible class leader, and so on.

STEP 2: INITIATE A FRIENDSHIP
Intentionally initiate a friendship with each woman on your list. If you're new to the church, or if you're delinquent in showing love to these leaders, check off that list as you take one to lunch each week for a while. Spend one-on-one time. Listen more than you talk. Hear her Christian story and her heart for ministry. Show your support for her ministry. Be enthusiastic about how God is working. Commit to pray for her. Chat about her family and interests, and learn from her.

When she mentions she adores chocolate, make a mental note. If she's taking a photo class, pay attention. If she's concerned about her mom's surgery, write down the date. Is her child in the high school play or on the city soccer team? Does she want to learn to play handball? Your goal is to know her more personally and show that you support her. When her birthday arrives, a minibox of fine chocolate tells her you listened. A simple prayer text the day before her mom's surgery, with an encouraging Scripture, will mean that you care.

This initial time investment can be a springboard to an ongoing friendship. Yes, you're both busy with your own friends, family, and ministries, but now she knows for certain that you love her and she can count on you. The friendship will impact both your lives positively. Never allow discord to come between you. It's likely your fellow staff couples will be lifelong treasured friends. Begin now.

You're both busy in different areas of ministry, so it may be infeasible to spend time with every staff wife or leader's wife regularly. That initial friendship launch, however, coupled with an encouraging word or cup of coffee together occasionally, can remind her of your support. You're not forming an exclusive, us-against-them friendship with staff members and leaders. Rather, you're demonstrating true fellowship. One quick way to destroy a church is to have squabbles or competition among the staff or leaders. It's important to the pastor and to the congregation that church staff members and leaders are a cohesive team with their pastor. The church family mirrors the church staff.

STEP 3: LOVE HER LIKE A SISTER

Acknowledge her value. Speak and call her by name when you see her. Compliment her sincerely. Brag about her to others. Appreciate her. Show respect with your words, body language, and attitude.

Help her excel. Encourage her giftedness. If she's new, help her fall in love with this missions field and find friends. Invest in her success.

Enjoy her. Try to grab some time together occasionally. Laugh together. Find something you have in common. Let church members "catch you" fellowshipping together.

Pray faithfully for her, and tell her you pray. Post a list of staff members or church leaders on your car visor to remind you to pray.

Love her children. Call them by name, and know something about each one. Speak to them. Encourage them. Do something nice for them occasionally. Your investment in your staff members' and leaders' children is priceless.

Minister to her. When crisis comes, be there first. When you come across a Scripture that might encourage her, text or mail it. Pay attention to milestones in her life, and help celebrate. A simple phone call or shared soda on her birthday can be meaningful.

> *This is my commandment: Love each other in the same way that I have loved you.*   JOHN 15:12

SHARE HOSPITALITY WITH CO-LABORERS

There's great value in fellowshipping together as couples or families, or as a staff or leadership group. It helps reinforce your love and acknowledge their value. Dedicate your house to God, and watch for opportunities to use it to honor Him.

Consider hosting a cookout for deacon families, a reception for Sunday School or small-group leaders, a lunch for ministry staff or volunteers, a gathering for new church members.

Don't be overwhelmed with the idea of hospitality. Hospitality doesn't have to be a six-course meal served on china. I'd never invite friends over if that was true! You might enjoy planning an occasional gathering for staff wives or other leaders. They'll love coming to your home for a family cookout in the backyard or a Christmas gathering to roast marshmallows in the fireplace. Serve chili for the deacons and wives. Invite some leaders for watermelon. Whether it's a full-fledged party or iced tea on the porch, relationships are grown when you practice hospitality.

Consider hosting an occasional gathering for wives of staff or leaders. Here's a simple plan I used for years: Two or three times each year, our staff wives would meet at my house for an appetizer. Then we'd hop in cars and make a very short ministry visit together before eating out at a restaurant. I'd prayerfully think of someone who needed special encouragement, such a newly widowed member or someone who just came home from the hospital. I'd call to ask if we could stop by for a five-minute visit. We'd all show up, hug her, and pray for her, then head out for dinner. It was a blessing to the staff wives as well as the recipient. There was no program or agenda at dinner. We'd catch up on one another's lives, laugh a lot, and leave better friends than before. Make it fit your group, and help friendships gel. Remember to take a quick group photo. You'll treasure those!

Hospitality takes effort. I met a pastor's wife in Cuba who loves to practice hospitality. When hosting guests in their tiny home, she and her husband walk to their church building to sleep on the pews. I think that's why Romans 12:13 (HCSB) instructs us to *pursue* hospitality. It's easier to get too "busy," but when we intentionally pursue those opportunities, relationships are enhanced.

Begin by inviting some leaders to your home this week. You'll be blessed more than you can imagine.

Show love to co-laborers who serve behind the scenes. Stop by a preschool Sunday School class and compliment the teacher. Take a sandwich tray to the office volunteers or administrative assistants. Express appreciation to the custodial volunteers or employees. Compliment the sound tech.

Show love to co-laborers outside your own church or ministry. Get to know other pastors' wives in the community, denominational leaders' wives, or a missionary your church supports. Those could be meaningful relationships.

Show love for co-laborers by intentionally mentoring younger women. It's surprisingly natural and easy, and it's God's plan for women (read Titus 2).

Of course, every church member is a co-laborer. Genuinely care about church members. The faithful ones, the occasional ones. The sweet ones and mean ones, rich ones, poor ones. The flamboyant ones and all those in between. Love them. Listen. Acknowledge them. Try to recognize them at the grocery store or restaurant and speak to them. Learn names, even if it's difficult. It means a lot to church members. Make notes if that helps you. Use a church directory or list to pray for them by name, and check each name as you pray. Share God's love verbally and in tangible ways, especially during crisis and celebration times.

"We call her 'the Glue,'" an Ohio deacon chairman said about his pastor's wife. "She connects us." A quiet-spoken woman, she simply loved the people and staff. She helped connect them in friendship and ministry. I glanced over the deacon's shoulder to see the pastor's wife, who had overheard his compliment. The Glue beamed.

Don't ever be overwhelmed with the privilege of loving co-laborers. It's a natural, one-day-at-a-time privilege. Watch for opportunities, and those relationships will develop over time. Love your co-laborers. Lavishly.

Encourage each other and build each other up.

1 THESSALONIANS 5:11

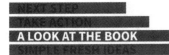

A COLLAGE OF CO-WORKERS

See Colossians 4:7–14. It's a blessing to have Christian sisters who co-labor with us in ministry. Paul describes several fellow workers in this Scripture. Open your Bible and read along. Compare those characteristics to your fellow workers, and write a few of their names on the lines below.

Tychicus, Paul's trusted and faithful friend; always available to meet needs.
- My trusted, available friend is: _____
- I am a trusted and available friend to: _____

Onesimus, whose name means "useful," is a faithful brother in Christ.
- My useful, faithful sister in Christ is: _____
- I am a useful, faithful sister to: _____

Aristarchus - a friend who's been through some hard times with Paul.
- My co-laborer who's shared hard times is: _____
- I am a friend who's there in hard times for: _____

Mark — Their relationship was breached, but now restored. Facing execution, Paul asked for him.
- My co-laborer, who I've forgiven and love as a sister: _____
- I am a forgiven and restored friend to: _____

Justus — a friend who always does right. He, along with Aristarchus and Mark, was a comfort to Paul.
- My righteous friend who comforts me is: _____
- I am a comforting friend to: _____

Epaphras — Paul's consistent prayer warrior.

■ My consistent prayer warrior is: _____

■ I am a consistent prayer warrior for: _____

Luke — Paul's loyal, constant companion who stood with him in good and bad times—missionary journeys, imprisonment, Paul's stoning and final imprisonment.

■ My loyal friend who shows genuine Christian love: _____

■ I am a loyal, loving friend to: _____

Demas — Paul's dear friend and co-laborer who later deserted him.

■ My co-laborer who's disappointed me: _____

■ I pray I won't desert my friends!

Archippus — a fellow pastor who Paul encouraged.

■ A fellow ministry wife who I've encouraged is: _____

■ I have been encouraged by this sister in ministry: _____

Aquila and Priscilla (cited later) — who corrected Paul in love, encouraged him in ministry.

■ My co-laborers who have corrected me in love and encouraged me are: _____

■ I am an Aquila/Priscilla-type, encouraging friend to: _____

_____

Paul mentions that Aristarchus, Mark, and Justus had been a comfort to him as fellow workers. *Comfort* is the Greek word from which we get our English word, *paregoric*. These fellow workers were like a soothing tonic to Paul.

In ministry and the Christian life, you need people who share the workload and are reinforcements for you. You need co-laborers who help lighten the burden and bring blessing to your life and ministry. Thank God for faithful Christian sisters.

Love My Co-laborers

List all of your ministry co-laborers and evaluate your relationship with each of them, using the following checklist. My Co-laborer's Names (Staff wife, leader's wife, etc.)

❑ I encourage her.

❑ I praise her privately and publicly.

❑ I know her Jesus story.

❑ I know her heart. Her needs.

❑ I take her to lunch occasionally.

❑ I know her kids' names and love them.

❑ I pray for her. I tell her I pray for her.

❑ I give her sincere compliments.

❑ I know her spiritual gifts.

❑ I acknowledge her birthday.

❑ I include her in conversations.

❑ I share ministry with her sometimes.

❑ I always speak well of her.

❑ I watch for ways to help her.

❑ I don't pretend I'm her boss.

❑ I don't talk to her hubby through her.

❑ I listen carefully when she speaks.

❑ I love her as a sister.

Love Your Missions Field

Have you fallen in love with the missions field God has assigned to you and your husband? Whether you've been there 30 years or 30 days, you can make an intentional effort to begin or restart a love affair with your missions field. Research it. Explore it. Get involved. Love it.

KNOW YOUR MISSIONS FIELD

When you take the time to learn facts, figures, and trivia, it demonstrates your commitment and love for your missions field. Become an expert on the town.

MISSION FIELD PRETEST

If you don't know for sure, make a guess and check it later.

Population: _____ County Population _____

Estimated % lost: _____

Average age of citizens: _____

school students _____

% unmarried adults _____

Ethnicity mix _____

Mayor's name: _____

High School mascot: _____

Elevation: _____

Avg summer temperature: _____ winter: _____

Your city's "claim to fame:" _____

Largest annual festival: _____

Top employers in town: _____

Someone famous who's from your town: _____

An unusual fact about your town: _____

State bird: _____ Time Zone _____

My favorite thing about our town: _____

Spend a little time this week doing research to increase your knowledge about the place where you serve God. Begin at census.gov, typing in your city name or ZIP code and learning interesting facts and stats. Gather brochures from the city hall and chamber of commerce. Comb community Internet sites. If you're not adept at computers, your local librarian can assist. You'll be amazed at what you can learn in a short time.

Care enough to learn the culture. Think about it: If you are going on an overseas missions trip, you'll carefully study that area's landmarks, people, and culture. If God has placed you in New York City or Slicklizard, Alabama, it's equally as important to know your missions field. For example, if God moves you to Indiana, you'll learn to play cornhole and Euchre, and to hunt and eat mushrooms. If He places you in Texas, you'll throw horseshoes and play 42, and avoid poisonous mushrooms. You may need to exchange "y'all" for "you guys," or "huh?" for "eh?" The wardrobe you wore in Fort Worth may need a tweak to fit in well in Los Angeles or Billings, Montana.

EXPLORE YOUR MISSIONS FIELD

Whether you're new or have served there for years, spend an hour this week to wander and discover. Buy a paper map and mark it up or use a phone app. Don't worry if you get lost while you explore; you can always use your GPS to get back home. Drive past interesting places you haven't been—parks, city building, hospitals, schools, historic sites. Be observant. Notice architecture, agriculture, culture, beauty. Observe people's faces and attitudes.

Pray as you drive. Ask God to use your explorations to give you a great love for your town, a compassionate heart for its people, and to inspire ideas for new ministry opportunities. Pray for people groups and students and businesspeople. Make notes so you can return to places that interest you. Walk inside the ethnic grocery store or the city hall. Sit in the park. Stroll downtown streets. New discoveries make this *your* home.

Learn about the church or ministry where you serve. Find out about its ministries, past successes, membership, and attendance numbers. Study every website page. If there's a printed history book, read it. Find a longtime or charter member, meet for coffee, and hear her story. Listen and learn. Ask members about longtime traditions and interesting facts. Walk through every room in the church. Study your church's denominational websites.

Learn about the people in your missions field. Study demographics. Learn about their education, income, ethnicity, family size. For example: If your missions field encompasses several ethnicities, your backyard barbecue should reflect that demographic. If a third of adults in your missions field are unmarried, pay attention to them. Be willing to get out of your comfort zone to reach people for Christ.

Learning about your city and church is enjoyable, and it will demonstrate your commitment to serving there.

"Here is a quote that we've have tried to live by in every ministry position that God has put us in. 'Wherever you are, be all there.'"
—*Corey Mescher (Mrs. Scott), Salado, TX*

EMBRACE YOUR MISSIONS FIELD

> *He decided beforehand when they should rise and fall, and he determined their boundaries.* ACTS 17:26

How would history have changed if Sarah told Abraham, "I just don't want to move away from Ur"? What if Lottie Moon had told God she'd serve Him, but only in Virginia, her home state? What if Ruth Graham had told Billy she didn't want him to travel? What if Kay Warren had told Rick she didn't want to plant a church with him?

I love learning stories about how God gave a ministry couple a heart for their specific missions field. I'm amazed how God strategically places chaplains, seminary professors, missionaries, and pastors. A missions assignment may not be glamorous, convenient, or comfortable. It may even be dangerous. When God calls you there, be obedient, and He will give you a love for that place and people. Rely on His calling and He will use you greatly. Serve Him there with joy and contentment.

For a decade I've watched as my friend Mary Ellen and her minister-husband relocated from their comfortable home and large church in the States to Ukraine. Serving as missionaries for the International Mission Board, they've fully invested their lives training church planters and pastors, and ministering to people who live in their apartment building and city. God has given then a great love for that missions field in a strategic, historic time. When they visit friends and family in the States, they can hardly wait to return.

You serve in a missions field. Join God fully there. Ask Him to give you a great love for that place and people, and then give it all you've got!

After a deacons wives' training conference, two ladies approached me for advice. They were thrilled about their church's new pastor and family. The church had welcomed them warmly, but the pastor's wife was unhappy. Her constant complaints were overwhelming. She disliked the weather. Her kitchen was too small. She missed her former church's women's group. And their town had no Starbucks. "What can we do?" they pleaded. "We can't change the weather!"

Sometimes, in the effort to be honest, we unintentionally give church members the impression it's their job to make us happy. Because you're the minister's wife, others may take your flippant complaints very seriously. Trust God's call. Speak positive words about your missions field. Ask God to give you love for the people and place He's assigned you. Invest yourself there. Make friends and memories. And if there's no Starbucks, brew a cup of Folgers.

Don't focus on negatives. My husband and I served as pastor and wife in a lovely town that had bothersome train tracks. It seemed everywhere I'd drive, I'd be delayed by train crossings. One day, as I sat silently irritated about the slow-moving train blocking my path, my young daughter gazed calmly at the slow-moving monstrosity. In her sweet little voice, she stated, "I love it when we get caught by a train, Mom. It gives us time to chat." Wow! What a difference in perspective! That day, I determined to find joy in the train-waiting moments. I'd allowed small inconveniences to smudge my contentment.

As a lifelong Texan, and a pastor's wife there for decades, you can imagine my apprehension about moving to serve in the Midwest. I was shocked and thrilled to find friendly people (they call it Hoosier hospitality), gorgeous four-season weather (I am now a huge snow and autumn fan), and a massive missions field I could never have imagined in America. The contrast between serving in a local church and a denominational ministry presented another huge adjustment. Because Steve's ministry would involve constant travel, we purchased a three-room condo in downtown Indianapolis and downsized sharply. Surprisingly, we quickly fell in love with our new lifestyle. I could give a downtown tour better than many natives, and God gave us a deep love for the urban and rural missions fields of Indiana.

A decade later, Steve's ministry with the North American Mission Board changed from working with the midwest states to the southern states. It was a perfect fit for his ministry gifts, and we're settled in a new missions field in beautiful Pensacola, Florida. I can honestly say that we have loved every missions field—hard or easy, large or small, hot or cold—that God has given us.

Joyfully remind your co-laborers that you're thankful to be on mission here. It may be difficult to move, but your trust in God will produce contentment.

HOW TO EMBRACE YOUR MISSIONS FIELD

- Subscribe to the local newspaper or online paper. Read it daily to know what's happening in your community.
- Become part of the community. Change your car's license plate and driver's license ASAP. If you've moved to a new state, remove bumper stickers marking you as an "outsider." Open an account at the local bank. Learn the butcher's name. Change your phone number to a local area code. Cheer for the local ball team and buy a T-shirt.
- Settle in. Improve your home's exterior appearance quickly. Plant a few bushes or flowers, or add fresh paint, and neighbors will notice. Consider buying a home. Nothing says, "We're staying" like a home investment.
- Meet the neighbors. Don't wait for them to come to you. Within a few days after moving in, stop to meet your ten nearest neighbors. As you knock, think these words: *longtime relationship* and *Do they know Jesus?*
- Observe cultural differences in your new setting. Pay attention, and make needed adjustments. For example, your wardrobe may need to change slightly in order to fit in.
- Get involved in the community. Explore the town. Volunteer. Take a class. Join a gym, service club, historical society, neighborhood organization, service club, or sports league. Attend a city council meeting, town festival, or high school ball game.
- It takes time to have longtime friends, so be intentional, and get started.

- As you meet new people, ask this question: Tell me, Sandy. What do you most love about Tippecanoe? Keep an ongoing list of responses.
- Find something you like about the church building. A pastor's child in Nederland, Texas, showed me "the longest pew in America" in their church balcony. A rural church we served during seminary had a church bell we rang with a rope each Sunday. I loved that!
- Say the words often: "I love Detroit." Tell your co-laborers you are glad to be here.

GET INVOLVED IN YOUR MISSIONS FIELD

Your everyday life will naturally lead to involvement in the community where you'll find evangelistic opportunities and create goodwill toward your church and your God. Need a starting spot? Learn and remember the names of your pharmacist, coffee barista, grocery checker, librarian. Be personable and friendly as you walk through life.

Your community involvement may be related to life stages. For example, if you have school-aged children, your largest influence may be in the public school. Befriend teachers and pray for them. Volunteer in the school office or library. Join the PTO or other organizations. Be a positive influence there. If there's a school carnival or field day, you're there—helping out, loving people, making friends. If you're a preschooler's mom, your largest community influence may be in the city park or the playgroup. A senior adult's missions field may be the red hat club or a place you volunteer in the community.

As you walk out the door each morning, view your first "missions field" outside your family. God has placed you in this neighborhood. Make a chart or use an app to list your closest neighbors, perhaps the units in your apartment building or homes on your block. Use an online reverse directory to gather names, and casually confirm them as you meet people. As you walk or mow or shovel snow, be friendly and helpful. Develop witnessing relationships. Pray for them. Talk about

God. God may prompt you to share a loaf of Christmas bread or plan an annual neighborhood Christmas tea, neighborhood cookout, or Easter egg hunt. Be aware of needs and crises in those families, and shine for Jesus.

If you work outside your home, your community involvement may be related to your employment. I loved my job as Main Street manager in our city's downtown area. I got to know many people I never may have met otherwise—downtown merchants, city council members, and town leaders. Little did we know 9/11 would happen. Our inner-city church hosted a citywide prayer meeting during that national crisis, and I invited work associates, including city leaders. They came in droves, and God used those work relationships and my pastor-husband to lead several to know Christ personally!

Whether God leads you to work as a homemaker, a professional career woman, a full-time volunteer or a part-time worker, God will use your work to His glory. Be very aware God has placed you there to shine for Him.

> *Obey your earthly masters with deep respect and fear. Serve them sincerely as you would serve Christ. Try to please them all the time, not just when they are watching you. . . . Work with enthusiasm, as though you were working for the Lord rather than for people.*
>
> EPHESIANS 6:5–6, 7

A church planter's wife once shared her philosophy of employment. "I absolutely love my job as a nurse," she glowed. "I feel God called me to that field, and I show His love to my patients. The income from my job also allows our family to contribute significantly to the budget and building fund for our church plant!" I was a real estate broker when we were planting a church. Clients were stuck in my car for days, so in addition to finding their dream home, my goal was to tell them about my amazing God. If they were believers, I'd convince them to help us plant a church. If they weren't, I'd share about Jesus. It was a perfect way to help grow a new church and God's kingdom.

Well over half the pastors in my church denomination are bivocational. Many could not accomplish their ministry without their spouse's employment. Thank God for work's blessings.

> *Now he uses us to spread the knowledge of Christ everywhere, like a sweet perfume. . . . And who is adequate for such a task as this?*
>
> 2 CORINTHIANS 2:14, 16

Be amazed and thankful that God has entrusted you to serve Him here. Loving your missions field is important. It's critical to your husband and children. It's important to God! Will you fall in love with the people, the town, and the ministry here? Work hard. Be content. And find great joy, as you love your missions field. Lavishly.

"Be content . . . wherever . . . whenever . . . whatever.
Paul was. See Philippians 4:1–13."

—LIZ TRAYLOR (MRS. TED), PENSACOLA, FL

NEXT STEP
TAKE ACTION
A LOOK AT THE BOOK
SIMPLE FRESH IDEAS **MY COMMITMENT TO GOD**

❏ I will renew my commitment to read God's love letters daily.
❏ I will conscientiously show lavish love for my God.
❏ I will convince my husband that he's the most loved man in the world.
❏ I will make a plan to show big-time love to the co-laborers God has given me.

❑ I will explore my missions field, and pray as I go.

❑ I will be thankful and content for the missions field where I serve, and love it lavishly.

❑ I will view my employment as a missions field.

NEXT STEP
TAKE ACTION
A LOOK AT THE BOOK
SIMPLE FRESH IDEAS

Pick a couple of these action activities to reinforce your study of "Simple Step #3: Love Lavishly."

❑ Find two consecutive hours you can spend alone. Gather supplies, turn off your cell phone ringer, and head to the park for the two-hour challenge (p. 46).

❑ Make a habit of always carrying a small New Testament in your handbag, or put a Bible app on your phone.

❑ Before tonight, read the entire Bible chapter of Song of Solomon, about courtship, marriage, and intimacy. It's just a few pages long.

❑ Memory challenge: "But the person who loves God is the one whom God recognizes" (1 Corinthians 8:3).

❑ Make a commitment to read God's love letter (Bible) within one year. Begin today. Enjoy a chronological Bible or a different Bible translation. If you travel far to work, consider an audio Bible app. Move a bookmark as you read, or select a reading plan. This year I'm using Professor Horner's reading system. Ready? Go!

❑ Make a list of all the things you love about your husband. Personality traits. Strengths. Physical attributes. Habits. Read the list to him.

❑ Try the elevator rule.

❑ Get your children involved in learning about your town. See sites they've never seen before. Stop at the highest point in the city, get out of the car, and pray for your family's missions field.

❏ Make a list of ways you enrich your husband and family's life. Read Proverbs 31:10–31, especially verse 11.

❏ *Questions to chat over with a ministry wife:

- How are you involved in your community?
- How can you begin relationships for the purpose of evangelism there?
- What's your secret about how to keep God in first place of your life?
- What types of things do you do to encourage your minister-husband?
- Share an idea you've used to increase relationships with co-laborers in ministry.
- How are you involved in your community for the purpose of ministry?

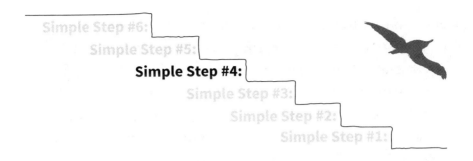

Simple Step #6:

Simple Step #5:

Simple Step #4:

Simple Step #3:

Simple Step #2:

Simple Step #1:

Say "We"

But the Holy Spirit produces this kind of fruit in our lives: . . . kindness.   GALATIANS 5:22

This fourth simple step may be the easiest, yet most profound discovery you've made in years. Practice saying this word aloud: "We."

We is such a powerful word! It says, "you and me"; "Let's"; "We're on the same team."

For a ministry wife, a simple change in attitude and terminology—from "I" to "we"—can totally revitalize your life.

Ministry is not a one-woman show. When she does everything in ministry alone—no matter how perfectly—others may view a minister's wife as aloof or uncaring. When a ministry wife overuses the pronoun *I*, she can easily be perceived as egotistical or selfish. But when she uses the team word *we* more often, attitudes change. Will you care enough about others to include them in ministry with you?

Think about the significance of the words *we, us,* and *our.* When a teacher talks about "our class" instead of "my class," the students

73

are drawn in and feel ownership. When a boss talks about "our team" rather than "me" or "my company," his employees feel invested. When a parent refers to his or her offspring as "our daughter" or "our son" as opposed to "my daughter," or "my son," it's apparent they are a family unit. John Glenn, astronaut and politician, was known for saying "we" rather than "I." Even Jesus' prayer focuses on "our Father," give "us" our daily bread, and lead "us" not into temptation.

Yes, the Christian life is very personal. My relationship with God is one-on-one, and can't be established without my own commitment and actions. However, God hasn't left us here on earth in a solitary vacuum. He established and blessed the union of two people—one man and one woman—in marriage. He created humans with the capacity for reproduction, resulting in family units. And He established and blessed the unifying, world-focused gathering of His people in the local church. Those three human relationships, marriage, family and church, benefit from a "we" mentality instead of an exclusive, self-focused "I" attitude.

That change in terminology, then, naturally lapses over into behavior and attitudes. When a ministry wife grasps the "we" aspect of her marriage, family, and church, she loses any semblance of selfishness or performance.

This is a big change. Begin a new habit of using the word *we* regularly, and put actions with those words. Even as you read this chapter, whisper the word aloud as you turn each page.

We the Couple

Does your church see you and your husband as a loving, cohesive ministry team? Do they view you as a supportive spouse to their pastor? Do they know you're crazy about one another? Your marital dynamic can be a great asset to your church's ministry. Let's talk about the ministry couple side of our marriage.

Why do so many pastor search committees include the ministry wife in the interview process? Because a pastor's wife can greatly inhibit or enhance his ministry. You can be his crown or his cancer.

> *"A worthy wife is a crown for her husband, but a disgraceful woman is like cancer in his bones."*
>
> PROVERBS 12:4

You are a child of God, serving Him with your own spiritual gifts. Your husband is serving God with his unique gifts as a pastor, or in another ministerial position. The two of you, bonded together in marriage, make quite a team. When your church views you as a unified team—separate, yet both dedicated to God and His church—God is honored. When you use the term *we* rather than *I* often, others see you as a cohesive team.

Though your personalities may be opposite, your God and your life purpose is the same. You are not competing with one another. You're not trying to be the pastor; you have your own responsibilities and ministries. You're not his employee or his boss. But you are a complimentary force and you're his best fan.

I once heard an elderly pastor's wife boast about her superiority over her husband. "Yes, he is the head of our household all right, but I am the neck. And the neck decides which way the head will turn!"

It's not culturally correct these days to allow the husband to be the leader in our homes, but it's absolutely biblical (see Ephesians 5:22ff.) Will you imitate the typical female on television, putting down the insignificant man in the room? Or will you choose God's plan? Be your husband's crown. His partner. His lover. His bride.

TIPS TO SHOW RESPECT TO YOUR HUSBAND
■ **Use body language to show respect for your husband.** Smile when he enters a room. Nod agreement. Listen when he speaks.

- **Teach your children to respect him.** No exceptions. Allow him to lead in marriage and family. Are your children acutely aware Dad is the leader?

- **Show him he's important to you.** When you get good or bad news, be sure he's the very first person you tell, even before posting it on Facebook or calling your sister or best friend. Look your best for him. Casual is fine, but good grooming and a little effort shows your love and respect, even on days off.

- **Depend on his wisdom. Ask his opinion.** Take his advice. Trust him. When you're with others, don't interrupt when he's talking. Show love and respect by listening attentively when he's preaching.

- **Treat him like a man, not a child.** Don't tell him what to do or correct his manners or stories in front of others. (If it's really important, tell him privately later.) Do you imitate the offensive woman in television commercials who belittles her man, or do you show lavish love by respecting him consistently?

- **Appreciate him.** When a wife is demanding or whiney, respect is not shown. Say thank you, sincerely and often. Treat him as your partner, not your servant. Appreciate him as your pastor too. Compliment his sermon and his leadership. Lean on him. Never let him doubt whether you're on his side.

- **Don't usurp his role as pastor.** Allow church members to view you as a supportive wife. He may ask your opinion about sermons or church decisions, and that's fine in private, but don't express your negative opinion to church members or in business meetings. Influence him with care. Be wise and prayerful with your input. Avoid manipulating him. Don't allow others to use you to get to the pastor, and don't appear to boss him. He reports to God, not to his wife. Ouch.

- **Be his best fan on earth.** Many average guys have excelled as great leaders or pastors partly because their wife believed in them.

Build him up. Make your husband look good; don't publicly list his shortcomings. This is not a pretense of perfection; it's respect. Don't belittle or talk negatively about him, even in jest. If you love him, and if you want to honor God, then every comment you make about him to others should be positive.

The clichéd saying "Two for the price of one" is often bantered about in ministry wives' complaint sessions. Here's my answer: I am a child of the King. If my husband were a garbage collector, I would still be totally involved in my church's ministry. My love for God and His church is not based on my husband's vocation. Being a ministry wife just enhances my opportunities for service. Oh yes, they get two for the price of one. Joyfully!

Enjoy talking about ministry together. Yes, there may be occasions when you need to declare a "no church talk" evening, but often, it's fun to dream big dreams and chat together about all God is doing.

Sometimes your biggest contribution to the partnership might be as a sounding board for your husband's dreams in ministry. Don't squelch or question his "crazy ideas" for ministry! Our husbands often need a safe place to dream big and crazy without someone saying, "Do you know how much money it would cost?" or "We don't have the staff to tackle something that big." He may need someone who will listen to him talk out those ideas, nod, ask positive questions to lead him to think deeper about it, and pray with him through it. Sometimes those big dream ideas are just the thing the church needs and your pastor-husband needs someone "on his side" as he begins expressing his vision to the church or staff.

Use the list below to prayerfully select a few favorite ideas for working as a ministry team with your husband. Use them as a catapult to demonstrate "we the couple" in your ministry setting.

"My jealousy seems to disappear whenever I join my husband in ministry rather than being resentful of the attention he gives the church."
—LAURA CHRISTOPHERSON (MRS. JEFF), TORONTO, CANADA

TEAM TIPS FOR THE MINISTRY WIFE

❑ Trust him.

❑ Respect him.

❑ Build him up.

❑ Enrich his life.

❑ Treasure him.

❑ Pray together.

❑ Be visible at church.

❑ Give him quiet time.

❑ Make him look good.

❑ Be his faithful friend.

❑ Pray for him faithfully.

❑ Listen when he speaks.

❑ Love the shoes you're in.

❑ Be his crown (Proverbs 12:4).

❑ Stand by him after church.

❑ Respect him as your pastor.

❑ Try to be up when he's down.

❑ Take sermon notes in a journal.

❑ Carry a few of his business cards.

❑ Have fun doing ministry together.

❑ Don't put him down, even in jest.

❑ Don't tell him how long to preach.

❑ Be his calm, trustworthy confidante.

❑ Tell him when you're proud of him.

❑ Create ministry memories together.

❑ Be his partner in life and in ministry.

❑ Always be an asset, never a liability.

❑ Don't critique him in front of others.

❑ Tell him you're glad he's your pastor.

❑ Pay rapt attention when he preaches.

❑ Watch for ways to be a blessing to him.

❑ Go out for ice cream after outreach visits.

❑ Cut him slack if it's an unusually hard week.

❑ Tell him you love being his ministry partner.

❑ Remember that he answers to God, not you.

❑ Be willing to be inconvenienced for ministry.

❑ Ask him for ideas how to better support him.

❑ Realize you're enjoying serving God together.

❑ Try to take pressure off him, not add pressure.

❑ When ministry demands are crushing, hug him.

❑ Be available to minister with him when needed.

❑ Let him be the pastor. You be the pastor's wife.

❑ Appreciate the privilege of serving God together.

❑ Don't compare him to another preacher-minister.

❑ Willingly go the extra mile on Sundays, especially.

❑ Appreciate his work ethic and heavy responsibility.

❑ Make life an adventure. Love the journey together.

❑ Be flexible. Be adaptable. Be content in all situations.

❑ Stop by his study before Sunday worship and kiss him.

❑ Build him up. Compliment him in private and in public.

❑ Ask him to pray for you before you go to work or sleep.

❑ Learn from him. Ask a question about your Bible lesson.

❑ Avoid greed or bitterness. Let him know you're satisfied.

❑ See ministry as a marriage enhancer, not as a competition.

❑ Pay attention when he talks, not interrupting or correcting.

❑ Sit together in church as a couple when he's not preaching.

❑ Be a good Christian example, in priorities, modesty, lifestyle.

❑ Be gentle with criticism, especially his sermons or leadership.

❑ Make a commitment to never come into worship service late.

❑ Don't try to be his "god." His top allegiance is to the Almighty.

❑ Never speak about him negatively to members, friends, parents.

❑ After Sunday worship, compliment something about his sermon.

❑ Keep his confidences. Let him talk without telling him what to do.

❑ About midweek, tell him something you learned from Sunday's sermon.

❑ Say "we" often.

Your relationship as a ministry couple is much bigger than "I." Say, "We the couple."

"Don't be discouraged when your husband is discouraged. Fake enthusiasm if you have to, but don't go into despair together!"

—LAURA SMITH (MRS. SCOTT), SOUTH BEND, IN

NEXT STEP
TAKE ACTION
A LOOK AT THE BOOK
SIMPLE FRESH IDEAS   **THE "WE" EXTERMINATOR**

2 Samuel 6:16–23. The quickest way to squelch the "we" factor in marriage is with criticism. In this Bible story, the villain is a critical wife.

King David was returning the ark of the covenant to Jerusalem. It was a grand day. Picture the scene—David and the entire house of Israel were celebrating before the Lord as they returned the ark. There was singing, and the sound of the ram's horn, and they were playing all kinds of musical instruments.

And there's King David, right out there in the middle of the street, rejoicing, dancing with all his might before the Lord. His wife, Michal, however, looked from her window with disgust at David, who was dancing and leaping before the Lord.

In *The Study Bible for Women*, Drs. Dorothy Patterson and Rhonda Kelley vividly expound:

> "Michal was more concerned with royal dignity than with spiritual authenticity and was embarrassed by David's behavior. . . . She accused David of improperly displaying himself in front of the crowds, even suggesting he had exhibited lewd behavior. Michal's words of hatred, jealousy, and preoccupation with others' opinions echoed Saul's (her father) attitudes. Michal, in turn, was humbled by the Lord, for she had no child to the day of her death, which for women at this time was considered a curse. David's heart, however, is revealed in his motivation for worshiping and glorifying the Lord."

Wow! Could that have been you or me? Has there been an occasion when you criticized your husband's overenthusiastic actions or words, but he was simply trying to please his God? Or a time when he came home jubilant and you squelched his joy? Have you ever been more concerned by what others would think than his heart's motivation?

Be careful with criticism. Your minister-husband needs his life partner to be the other half of "we the couple." He needs an encourager, not another critic.

We the Family

Children born to a young man are like arrows in a warrior's hands. How joyful is the man whose quiver is full of them!   PSALM 127:4

Steve and I were married seven years before our first son, Tylor, was born, so I was more than delighted to finally be a "happy mother of children" (Psalm 113:9). Our two sons and daughter are now adults, married to awesome spouses, and we have three grandchildren.

> *Children are a gift from the LORD; they are a reward*
> *from him.*　　　　　　　　　　　　　　　　PSALM 127:3

Parenting is one of life's greatest joys. There's nothing more fun, more humbling, or more rewarding than being a parent. How can parents, and specifically a ministry couple, provide a healthy home life and help their children to enjoy loving and serving God? How can we create that "we the family" dynamic?

My husband, Steve, served as director for our denomination's state office, and we had traveled a few hours that Sunday to one of our churches. After enjoying a wonderful worship service, we took the pastor and his family to the local restaurant for lunch.

I froze when the pastor asked his young teenage boy to voice the prayer for our food. Would that embarrass him? But with no hesitation, he prayed to his God. I'll never forget that long lanky teenager's prayer. One sentence almost drew me to tears. He whispered, with feeling, "God, I thank You so much for the awesome sermon my dad preached today." It wasn't braggadocious or ingratiating. He was truly appreciative of how God used his dad that morning.

Another Sunday in another town, I sat in a church lobby, waiting for Steve to finish with a meeting. A young boy, obviously waiting on his parent, wandered over and sat nearby. After a silent moment, he volunteered, "See that door?" I looked at a huge wooden door that led into the worship area, unsure how to respond to his odd question. He continued matter of factly, but proudly, "I helped carry that door." That pastor's kid knew he was part of the ministry team. When they built the church building, he and several men had helped carry the door.

"We the family" means we're not only committed to loving and serving one another, but we also have a joint goal to love and serve our God together. When your entire family catches the vision, everything changes. The children see their own value to God's plan. Inconveniences are less bothersome.

I remember sitting in the living room floor with our kids to discuss a potential move from our beloved church to a new place of ministry across the state. They were in fifth grade, seventh grade, and ninth grade. Steve and I felt God was leading us to the new pastorate, but were still praying through our final decision. We confided in our children, asking their input, since this would be an enormous change.

I've never been so surprised and so proud. One by one, our children affirmed the potential life change with great faith and bravery. One said, "Well, if that's where God wants us, let's go!" They were packing before we even decided. We certainly weren't asking our children's permission, but their understanding of God's call on our entire family was humbling.

Let's discuss three actions that can prompt that "we the family" conviction: setting priorities, discipleship, and serving with joy.

SET FAMILY PRIORITIES

> As for me and my family, we will serve the LORD.
>
> JOSHUA 24:15

There's that *we* word again. Our overarching priority as a family is to honor and serve God. Everything else in our lives is built around that single purpose. Work with your husband to write a brief family priority statement with that focus, describing your family priority of serving God. The statement can be a sentence or two long.

Print your statement, with your family name in large letters at the page's top and Joshua 24:15 printed at the bottom. Frame it, and hang it in a visible place, such as the kitchen, laundry room, or garage entrance.

By posting the statement, each family member will be reminded to keep God at the center. As parents, we're busy providing basic needs—meals, clean clothes, housing, providing a home with warmth, security, and love. The posted statement can help us remember our top priority.

My parents were committed Christians, and modeled godly living. Each time I'd leave the house, I would remember my dad's words: "Remember whose you are!" I knew my actions reflected on the Matheus family, but that's not what Dad meant. Instead, he was reminding me I represent the King of kings. Although I might not represent Him perfectly, that stated goal certainly impacted my words and actions. Even a child is aware about his or her Christian influence. When goals are set before children, it's much more likely they will attain them.

A family priority statement simplifies future decision making. Our son's ball team had a playoff game rescheduled for a Sunday morning. It was only a one-time thing, and it was an important game, but he recognized it was a decision that would put sports above worshipping God. He didn't even hesitate, and respectfully told the coach he wouldn't be able to play. Surprisingly, his coach had the game rescheduled to another day, and the team decided to come to our church and sit together that Sunday! Because we had made a family commitment ahead of time, our child had no problem knowing priorities.

A family priority statement helps focus our worship. It's easy to slip into busyness without acknowledging its God-given purpose. We might even redirect our worship away from God. For example, we absolutely love our children; however, our precious child is not worthy of our worship. When our childrearing morphs into child worship, that child becomes an idol. Have you fallen into living life through your kids instead of living with them? Does your child feel he or she is more important than God? Do you talk more about your kids than your God? Let the world know you love your children, but be cautious to never give the impression you worship them. Worship is reserved only for God.

Your family priority statement impacts how you view every activity in life. It impacts how your family interacts with neighbors, friends, relatives, teammates, acquaintances, strangers. It affects how you spend money, use free time, and make decisions. Realize there's enormous quality in time spent together serving God in everyday life. Enjoy teamwork as a purposeful family and see how ministry intersects with friendships and family. You're a family on mission for God!

"Never tell your children, 'We have to go to church.' Instead say, 'We get to go to church!' They will pick up on the positive instead of the negative. Never tell your children they can't do such and such because they are the preacher's kid. Could they do it if they weren't the PK?"
—Dana James (Mrs. Ernie), Greenwood, IN

Give your children a stable, loving, uplifting home. Create a place where they feel safe to talk about anything. Work to make home a place they'll love to be and where they enjoy bringing others.

Treasure time with your family. Relish every stage of parenting. Share family meals, and make them pleasurable and revitalizing. Snatch minutes or hours to relax or work together. Plan memorable vacations and family events. Acknowledge that Christian ministry is truly a life work. Your family still experiences love when someone joins you for dinner. Ministry doesn't stop when you're at the city festival or grocery store. It expands there.

DISCIPLE YOUR CHILDREN

This may be the most important assignment of your life. You may disciple many people over the years, but don't neglect teaching your own child about God. "Direct your children onto the right path, and when they are older, they will not leave it" (Proverbs 22:6).

Discipleship involves both intentional teaching and intentional modeling. From your child's birth, begin to tell him or her about God. Delight your preschooler with stories from the Bible. Help your child hide God's Word in his or her heart. (I just watched a video of my three-year-old grandnephew, Cooper, quoting the fruit of the Spirit.) Teach your teen to research God's answers to life's questions using a Bible concordance and commentary. Make it fun and enticing. Pray together as a family about needs. Praise God together when He answers.

> *Watch out! Be careful never to forget what you your-self have seen. Do not let these memories escape from your mind as long as you live! And be sure to pass them on to your children and grandchildren.*
>
> DEUTERONOMY 4:9

Make an age-appropriate plan for teaching God's principles to your child, but also let your children "catch" you reading God's Word daily. Live a Christian life in front of your children. As your children observe your daily life, they are learning how to handle life's challenges God's way. They're learning modesty and manners and the fruit of the Spirit. They're learning to share, to keep promises, to look in the Bible for life answers. They're learning how to pray and trust God, and thank Him when He answers prayer. They're learning how to treat poor people, unkind people, friends, family members. Your children are watching and listening. They are being discipled by you. Psalm 101:2 reads, "I will live a life of integrity in my own home."

Be ready to introduce your child to Christ as personal Savior. My daughter decided she wanted to accept Jesus as her Lord in the parking lot of a restaurant one day. Eternity was changed and angels sang, right there in our van! Discipleship often happens as you're walking through everyday life with your family.

"The enemy has a target on the backs of the pastor's family. Don't give the enemy an open window." —BECKY OSBORNE (MRS. RON), DALLAS, TX

Help your child develop a personal, growing relationship with God. They need education and exercise, extracurricular activities and dinner, and so many things, but more than anything, they need a vibrant friendship with God. They may fail miserably, but they'll always have that foundation of Jesus to return to.

As they mature, teach your children to live in the real world by walking and talking them through things they see in the world as opposed to keeping your child in isolation so they never see anything outside your family. We all know ministry kids who went off to college and, for the first time in their lives, experienced the world. Many buckle because they've had no experience in handling it. Teach your kids how to stand up for what's right, but to have a perspective that understands others around them. As they mature, let them stay at a friend's house overnight. Don't bail them out of everything immediately. Give your child a chance to get their hands and feet a bit dirty so they can see their need for God.

Your goal is to train up a future adult who knows and serves God. You won't be with your child every moment of life. God will.

Help your children discover their spiritual gifts and use them in the church. Serving God isn't only for adults. Carefully observe your child's natural talents and interests. Appreciate his or her uniqueness. Watch for ways your children can use their spiritual gifts, then celebrate how God blossoms those gifts. Living for God is what every Christian does every day—even a child!

"My children love to go church! We show our enthusiasm for God, and involve them to participate in ministry such as singing, memorizing verses, and reward them for their effort."

—Katherine Santiago Gaspar (Mrs. Emilio),
Indianapolis, IN (Note her use of "we!")

Give your child a heart for missions. Allow him or her to give special missions offerings. Help your child know he or she is an important part of the missions assignment in your local church. Introduce him or her to Christian leaders. When a guest speaker or missionary is in your home, don't send the kids away. Instead, help them plan a question or two to ask. Encourage your guest to tell some stories about how God works. Then, according to your child's age, let them go play with their Legos. A three-minute conversation may impact your child's life forever.

Take your child on an age-appropriate missions trip. Yes, they can serve God at home, but a planned missions trip can be life changing. We took our children on missions trips in our local area, in North America, and overseas. God used those trips to help give them a heart for the world. They learned about other cultures. They appreciated their own home more than before. They met people who were different than them. They shared about Jesus. They found missionary friends, and prayed faithfully for them.

Teach your child to share his or her faith with others. It's natural for a God lover to tell others about Him. Don't stifle your child's enthusiasm for telling friends about God. Your child may be the most vibrant witness in your family.

Help your child to be considerate. Instead of making a "gimme" list for Christmas, help them make a list of what they'd like to give others. Make fun projects of helping others.

By watching you and your husband, your children are learning to love God's church and His people. Set the pace for "we the ministry family's" attitude about church members. We hear stories of church members serving "roast pastor" for Sunday lunch, yet we may serve "roast deacon"! When your children hear complaints and negative stories about those in your church family, it's likely they'll dislike them too.

Protect your children—especially your teens—from church gossip and problems. It's easier to gloss over things with smaller children, but your teenagers take every comment to heart. Amp up the "protective mom mode" around your teenager when it comes to problems and gossip in the church. Let your children see your consistent love for God's people.

As you anticipate Sunday worship, they anticipate Sunday worship. As you sincerely worship your Savior, they desire that great Lord. Help your children have their own love for God to take with them through life when they leave the nest.

Our daughter, Autumn, was a new freshman at Baylor University. She'd scoured her freshman dorm looking for someone who'd go to church with her on Sunday. There were lots of PKs and DKs (deacons' kids) in her hallway, but she had no luck. She called home, moaning. "They all seem to hate the church," she said. "Thank you for teaching me to love the church." Disastrous results await if you freely dump church problems on the children. Protect them.

"Guard the hearts of your children. Love and protect them."
—Christell Tallent (Mrs. Tim), Hartsville, IN

DISCIPLINE YOUR CHILDREN

Discipleship and mothering also involves discipline. How does a ministry wife handle discipline with her children?

Church members and other moms may be overly observant of a ministry wife as she disciples and disciplines her children. Don't let it fluster you! Simply be the best mom you can be, with God's guidance.

You'd be doing that whether you were the ministry wife or not, correct? Other parents may sometimes take their cues in parenting from you, so pray for great wisdom from God. Have high expectations for your children.

God's Word instructs us to discipline our children with love. Don't repeat old clichés about bad preachers' kids, or discuss your children's faults with others in front of them. We don't behave because Daddy is a preacher, but because we need to please God.

Be the parent. Don't leave your children to raise themselves. You can't parent by text or phone; be there. Your children don't need you to be a buddy; they need a mother. Expect a lot. Trust them; but parent them well. Say yes when you can, but be firm with your no. God gave you this privilege and important responsibility. For example, if there's no adult at home with a houseful of teens (or preschoolers), there's more likelihood of problems. If a mom doesn't teach and model modesty, it's likely her daughter won't learn God's teaching about modesty.

Observe Christian parents you admire, and ask their wisdom. Read Christian parenting books, enjoy positive blogs and parenting seminars, but compare every piece of advice with God's Word. Pray nonstop. Your child needs your guidance and discipline in daily life. Ask the Holy Spirit for guidance for each situation. You're preparing your child for adulthood. Take it seriously.

"Don't lose sleep about what church members think about your husband or children. You can't please everyone. Please God."

—DEBBIE WHIDDEN (MRS. MITCH), HOBART, IN

Psychologist James Dobson's updated books *The New Dare to Discipline* and *The New Strong-Willed Child* are great resources, and there are many quality parenting books with Christian teachings. When Dobson's first books came out, our children were preschoolers, and it seemed he'd been peeking into our home. His advice to "shape the will but don't break the spirit" became my theme song during those years.

When our preschooler, third-grader, teenager, or adult child fails, we don't give up. Our children aren't perfect, but neither are we! Allow your child to bear the consequences, but gently restore in love. Don't pretend your children are perfect, but be careful to never make them into public spectacles because they're the minister's kids. Then keep on lovingly discipling and disciplining. God loves your child even more than you do.

Let's be real, though. If there are kids running past microphones in the worship center's platform, they shouldn't be yours! Discipline matters.

A FOUR-STEP DISCIPLESHIP PLAN FOR PARENTS

DEUTERONOMY 6:5–9. Help! How can we find time to actually disciple our children? Here's great news. There's an awesome four-step teaching plan for parents found in Deuteronomy 6.

> *"And you must love the Lord your God with all your heart, all your soul, and all your strength. And you must commit yourselves wholeheartedly to these commands that I am giving you today. Repeat them again and again to your children. Talk about them when you are at home and when you are on the road, when you are going to bed and when you are getting up. Tie them to your hands and wear them on your forehead as reminders. Write them on the doorposts of your house and on your gates."*

Step 1: FIRST YOU (vv. 5–6). Before you give instruction to your child, commit wholeheartedly to God and His teachings yourself. There must be no doubt to your children about your love for God and His commands.

Step 2: REPETITION (v. 7). Repetitively teach God's commands to your children. Make an age-appropriate plan, using repetition to imprint them into their young minds. Be diligent in your teaching. Mesmerize preschoolers with exciting Bible stories. Help your children to memorize Scripture and learn to study the Bible for themselves. To bring them up in the training and instruction of the Lord, we must understand this is not a one-time lesson. Repeat.

Step 3: WHEN AND WHERE (v. 7). Discipleship is what happens during normal conversation—at mealtimes, leisure hours, any time. It occurs when you're at home and when you're on the road. It happens at bedtime, and first thing in the mornings. It's an ongoing teaching and modeling process, at all times and all places in life, relating discipleship to everyday situations. Take every opportunity to instill knowledge about God. During a walk, observe God in nature. Use travel time to talk about God. When you put kids to bed, pray together. Let them go to sleep considering God's greatness. Begin each new day with God.

Step 4: REMINDERS (vv. 8–9). Frontlets and phylacteries were small boxes worn on the Jews' forehead and wrists. There would be some Scripture verses inside, written on small rolled parchments, making God's Word easily available. Today, God's Word may be as close as our cell phone or a small New Testament in a handbag. Find ways to keep Scriptures in front of your children. My daughter once told me she'd memorized all the Scriptures I put on metal plates on mirrors and framed Scripture art in our home. Verse 9 suggests putting God's Word on our home's doorposts and entry gates, where outsiders can easily observe as they pass by. We the family want to be sure outsiders will observe His teachings in our home.

LET THERE BE FUN

If God has blessed you with children, help them to enjoy life as a PK. Help your child appreciate the many special privileges of being a minister's kid. Perhaps there's a church bell they can ring occasionally. Steve had a snack drawer in his office, and our kids were allowed to raid it. A church member once asked our young son, "What's the best thing about being the pastor's son?" His immediate response was, "Oh, I get to help turn on the baptistery water on Saturdays."

I've quizzed my grown kids about their thoughts about PK advantages. They knew how to converse with people of all ages. They got to travel on missions trips to many places. They each received a $10 bill from Mr. McClung (a former PK) at least once a year. During high school, a deacon arranged for our golfer son, Tylor, to play in a pro-am with Tom Kite. Justin remembered closets full of M&M's and Diet Dr Peppers, when church members bombarded their pastor with favorite snacks on an anniversary. Help your children appreciate little extra benefits.

It's possible for PKs to enjoy their role a little too much. I still recall our four-year-old son, encircled by some elderly church ladies who adored him, explaining how mistreated he was because his mother didn't make pumpkin pies. Justin had tasted it at Mother's Day Out, and it was yummy. Sure enough, the next Sunday, he proudly left church with four homemade pumpkin pies!

Other things take a few decades to figure out. Stories like poking holes in baptistery boots and Lord's Supper plastic cups, and shooting spitballs at sleeping Mr. Jones during church surfaced after our children became adults.

Begin simple traditions, such as doughnut shop breakfast Sunday mornings, "Sunday night candy" at the convenience store on the way to evening service, slow cooker roast and veggies for Sunday lunch. Celebrate their baptism with a party for everyone who's influenced your child. Snap photos to document your child's Christian activities and ministries. Bring friends from church to your home often to help develop relationships. Help your child know some older folks for friendship and ministry. Make any torturous event for a child (such as weddings) better by stopping for ice cream afterward.

The fun of being a kid and a family provides a natural way to show Jesus' joy to others. As the family walks through everyday life, they also enjoy ministry in their community. If kids are in T-ball, parents are automatically doing "bleacher ministry." Their children's schools provide amazing ways to impact lostness. A family touches their neighborhood, their friends, and their church. Whether they're playing at the playground, bowling in a city league, buying groceries, going to the high school ball game or city festival, they enjoy life as a family and, at the same time, find opportunities to minister to others.

Treasure your family, enjoy life and ministry with your family, and have fun.

"If hospitality extends to my family, it will naturally extend to others. Check out Proverbs 31."
—ALYSON WITT (MRS. JIM), GARLAND, TX

NEXT STEP
TAKE ACTION
A LOOK AT THE BOOK
SIMPLE FRESH IDEAS **TEN *WE* ENHANCERS**

- Wash your husband's car and leave a signed love note on the front seat.
- Plan a staycation day to show the kids sights around your town.
- Be the first person to volunteer at church, when God prompts.
- Accompany your husband for a ministry visit sometimes.
- Put a great photo of your husband on your desk or computer screen.

- Teach your child your favorite Bible verse today.
- Put the phone numbers for key women leaders in your cell phone for emergencies.
- Take a family photo in front of the church every Easter.
- Take a photo of your husband in the pulpit each church anniversary.
- Frame a family photo for your husband's desk at work.

The time is short. A typical woman's childrearing days engulf less than a third of her adult life. It's worth every short night or tear. Treasure every moment of motherhood. As you rear your children, and as you pray together and live together, use the word *we*. When they realize ministry isn't just what Dad does when he goes to work, your children can joyfully serve God themselves.

We the Church

How can a ministry wife intertwine her life with her church family or ministry assignment? Say "we the church" with your words, and add "we" actions to demonstrate you are a part of the church. Whether you've served in the same church for decades or newly arrived, it's important for the ministry wife to demonstrate her love for God's people and His work there.

NINE EASY WAYS A MINISTRY WIFE CAN CONVEY WE THE CHURCH

#1. Join. If you're new to your ministry assignment, move your church membership to your new church as quickly as possible. Join a small group. Join the women's group or the ball team. Joining will jump-start your relationship as we the church.

#2. Change your terminology. When a ministry wife embraces the concept of community, her influence is expanded. If you are a new church staff member's wife, your new terminology will be "our church" rather than "your church." If he serves with the state denominational office, you'll refer to "our churches" and "our state." If he's a military chaplain, it's "our base" and "our soldiers." When you take ownership and pride in your missions field, those you serve are validated and treated as partners.

God has carefully assigned your current place of ministry, and it's important to convey your peace and commitment to serve there. From the very first day you and your husband begin this ministry, change your terminology. Ask, "What time does our church's worship begin?" instead of "What time does your church's worship begin?" Avoid constant references to your previous ministry or your friends in faraway places. Don't unintentionally give the impression your desire is to go back "home." Give priority to your current ministry assignment. It's tempting to return to a former church to perform every wedding or funeral, but that is destructive for their new pastor's ministry. Keep those dear friendships, but plant yourself where God has assigned you.

"We" changes the aura of the church from watching its leaders to a biblical concept of a church body. It takes the focus off the pastor and pastor's wife. Ministry is not about you, as a leader, but points only toward God. Using the word *we* helps to create unity and a team mentality. It changes how others perceive you.

There's energy in *we*. There's mentoring in *we*. There's strength in *we*. There's community in *we*.

#3. Show up. Let them see you at church. This doesn't mean you need to sit on the platform or stand and bow, but your presence means a lot to your church and to your husband. It says "we the church."

You can't attend every happening at a growing church, but you can make the effort to be present for all-church gatherings and important events and ministries. And, of course, you'll be vibrantly involved in any specific ministry God assigns you.

Sunday worship really counts. Review the fourth commandment, and Hebrews 10:25 about not forsaking the assembling of yourselves. Your physical, joyful presence in worship demonstrates your commitment to we the church. Your commitment to worship may impact the employment you seek. It may negate your interest in travel sports teams for your child. As a leader, you give Sundays to God.

Determine how you can best use your time, and what works best where you minister. For example, as our church grew, it became overwhelming to try to attend social gatherings for every small group or team, but Steve and I would attend every Christmas celebration. We'd go from party to party, loving people and celebrating with them. Yes, it was a big effort, but over the years it became a fun tradition.

Find a way to balance family and church ministry. For example, when we served in a large church, bridal and baby showers became almost overwhelming during spring months. In that setting, the pastor's wife's presence was meaningful. I would often take a short break from family for a "drive-by" shower. (Oh, I would never repeat that phrase to a church member!) I'd pull on a skirt, drive to the church, and walk through the group, sipping punch and speaking to folks. Then I'd hug the bride, tell her I just wanted to stop by for her big day, and be back home with the family in only a few minutes. You may have to get creative, but joyfully show up when it counts.

One of the twelve disciples, Thomas . . . was not with the others when Jesus came.   JOHN 20:24

#4. Be friendly. In preparation for this book, I talked with dozens of active church members in different states, asking the simple question, What's the most important advice I could give a pastor's wife in this book? Most of their answers related to being friendly. They would say, "Speak to people" or "Be nice to people" or "Let us know you like us."

It's extremely important for any ministry wife—no matter her personality—to learn to be friendly. Your church members or ministry partners want to love you. They desire your success. And it means the world to them if you say their name and share a smile or kind word. If your personality is introverted, that's great news. Most people will respond even better to you.

I've noticed a common denominator among many ministry wives who serve in growing, effective churches. I call it the friendly factor. No matter the size church, those ministry wives seem to know almost everyone. They're intentional about showing God's love to as many people as possible every Sunday. They may not be extremely outgoing, but they're extremely friendly. This is not rocket science! We can do this. Be friendly.

"Speak to people, make an effort to remember names, smile and be cheerful, sit in different places in the sanctuary during worship services." —JEANETTE DRIGGERS (MRS. CARLISLE), EATONTON, GA

#5. Be an ambassador. Like it or not, a minister and his wife represent their church or ministry from the first day they arrive. It's a little intimidating, but everywhere you go, you represent your God (like every other Christian.) You also represent your church and your husband, the pastor or minister.

You don't need to wear a billboard to be recognized. This doesn't mean you need to wear a business suit to the beach. It simply means you'll consistently live like a Christian. You'll be extremely kind to restaurant servers. You'll drive the speed limit. You'll look presentable. You'll write emails or blogs with enormous discretion. You'll dress with unquestionable modesty. You'll speak with kindness and integrity.

Embrace your unofficial ambassador role and do it well. Being an ambassador does have its benefits. You get extra opportunities to shine for Christ. Say "we" as you represent your ministry.

#6. Stay off the pedestal. It's rare, but there are a few ministers' wives who feel their role should afford them special status in the world. They expect a monetary discount or a front row seat. They want to wear the fanciest clothes. They hint for gifts. They want people to pay attention when they enter the room.

A ministry wife's job description does not include pedestal posing. Pedestal posers expect special treatment and constant acknowledgment. They're sometimes overoccupied with collecting compliments and material possessions. They may behave as if it's the church members' job to keep them happy.

Don't be a prima donna pastor's wife! Pride leads to disgrace. Instead, be a servant leader. If you climb up and stand on a pedestal, you have further to fall. Never forget that your calling is not to shine for yourself, but to shine for Jesus. Say "we."

Our missions trip in Italy ended with a sightseeing day, and our teenage daughter was having a blast. At each monument or museum, she would pose a different person in our group for a funny photo. One beautiful garden had a long row of statues perched on pedestals, but one statue was missing. Autumn drug Mrs. Stephens to the vacant pedestal and convinced her to pose like a statue for her photo.

It was hilarious! She could only stay on the pedestal a few seconds before losing her balance, and the whole group was rolling with laughter. The photo was a keeper, but the lesson was valuable too. It's really hard to stand on a pedestal. Why try?

Care for the flock that God has entrusted to you. Watch over it willingly, not grudgingly—not for

> *what you will get out of it, but because you are eager*
> *to serve God.*　　　　　　　　　　　　1 PETER 5:2

#7. Include others in ministry with you. Chapter 6 is dedicated to helping find your own personal ministry, but when you include others with you as you serve, that says "we the church." If you're making a hospital visit or outreach contact, invite someone to accompany you. Invite a leader or a sideline church member to help you with a church project. Model how to do ministry. Get to know her. Stop for coffee together afterward. It takes little extra effort to share ministry. What does that accomplish? Bonding. Friendship. Teamwork. Discipleship. Multiplied ministry. Yes, you could certainly do that visit or ministry project on your own, but when you intentionally include others, you are demonstrating God's plan for the church family to function as a body of believers. We the church. By the way, this is called *mentoring*.

I absolutely love Vacation Bible School (VBS). Over the years, I've seen how God can use VBS to change many lives. Children and entire families get saved. VBS teachers rediscover the fruits of teamwork, evangelism, fellowship, and sacrifice.

Almost every year, I direct a fifth-grade VBS department. I gather a new teaching team, specifically seeking out church members who've never taught VBS. They are new church members, peripheral members, and other unlikely recruits. My goal is to have a wide range of ages and interests, and half male and female leaders (fifth-grade boys need great male Christian role models). We plan voraciously and pour ourselves into creating the best spiritual week of those kids' lives.

At our evaluation meeting, I challenge those teachers to lead out as a director for a different age group at VBS next year, and I begin to gather a new group of leaders to mentor. Whatever your ministry, make a great effort to mentor others as you serve. One great joy of being a pastor's wife for me has been helping others discover the joy and ease of serving God.

"Encourage others to value themselves and what they bring to the kingdom of God. As a ministry wife, remember you don't need to do everything. Encourage others, and let your light shine."
—VANESSA FLETCHER (MRS. REGINALD), INDIANAPOLIS, IN

#8. Connect them. Nothing says "we" like helping new and peripheral church members find friends and a place to serve. You are in a unique position to help that happen. Introduce people who have similar interests to one another. Invite potential friends to join you for lunch and help them connect. As you meet and fellowship with church members, listen intently. Ask probing questions about their interests, then help to connect their talents and spiritual gifts to ministry in the church. There's a true sense of "we" when every church member has a function (1 Corinthians 12:12–31; Ephesians 4:16).

When new members joined our church, they were invited to eat Wednesday night church dinner at the pastor's table. It provided a perfect opportunity for us to know them better and help them find a place to serve in the church.

"Don't be afraid to have friends in the church. One of the worst pieces of advice I ever received was not to be good friends with church members."
—SARAH BOHRER (MRS. JIM), BROWNSBURG, IN

#9. Have friends at church. Wait! Is a ministry wife allowed to have friends within her church or ministry group? You're going to love this answer.

Absolutely, yes! A ministry wife needs friends within her ministry setting! True ministry is all about relationships. This important verse, written by Paul, describes his relationship with Christians in his church:

> *We loved you so much that we shared with you not only God's Good News but our own lives, too.*
>
> 1 Thessalonians 2:8

Scripture instructs Christians to show family affection to one another; to serve one another; to be kind, tenderhearted, and forgiving to one another. We are to agree wholeheartedly with each other, and work together with one mind and purpose. It says we should motivate and help and encourage each other. We're to break bread together, pray for one another, share with each other in need. More than a dozen times, Scripture instructs us to love one another. All that sounds a lot like friendship to me!

> *A wise person wins friends.*   Proverbs 11:30

> *I am a friend to anyone who fears you—anyone who obeys your commandments.*   Psalm 119:63

Because you are a ministry wife, you likely have dozens or even hundreds of fringe friends. Many church members would consider you a dear friend. That's great! The reality, though, is you can't be a close friend with every person in your church. Be friendly with every church member and guest, but search carefully for a few ladies with whom you'll develop a closer relationship.

Jesus did that. He called many people "friend," and He truly loved the masses. Yet He surrounded Himself with a few dear friends. He spent time with them. He invested in them. The Apostle Paul often referred to members of his churches as his "dear friends."

How do I choose my closest friends? Comb Scripture and use common sense. Watch for women whom you connect with. Some parameters are obvious. Your best friend should be female. (Not counting your hubby here.) She should not be the church gossip or troublemaker, because you are known by your friends. She may be a woman who's in the background, or a leader in your church. It's desirable to have a friend who is modest, fun to be around, and brings you up a notch when you're around her. You may even have additional Christian friends who are members in another church.

Your dearest friends may be your age, or much younger or older. As a pastor's wife, I've always tried to find at least one good friend in each general age group. This is easily accomplished through mentor relationships. Be a friend collector! Always be on the lookout to make a new friend.

> *These older women must train the younger women to love their husbands and their children, to live wisely and be pure, to work in their homes, to do good, and to be submissive to their husbands. Then they will not bring shame on the word of God.* Titus 2:4–5

Yes, a ministry wife should have dear friends at church. Find them. Love them. Have fun with them. Minister with them. Minister to them. Enjoy them. Share life and God's blessings. Treasure them, but . . . here are *three very important cautionary warnings.*

WARNING: UNCLIQUE

Avoid any hint of a clique. This is adult life—not junior high. A ministry wife can have close friends without giving the appearance of an exclusive group. This means you and your friends don't walk around in a huddle at church, or tell private jokes or whisper to one another.

A clique could even happen among ministry staff wives! Your goal is to illustrate we the church, not we the Three Musketeers.

To avoid clique-ishness, I'd rarely sit by dearest friends in worship or church fellowships. I could see them during the week, but on Sundays I needed to be meeting guests, helping with ministry, getting to know other people, and chatting with the lonely or hurting people. If your friend's goal is to be "seen" with the minister's wife, find a different friend.

For example, the wives of our state denominational leaders were dear friends. It was no secret we loved one another. At statewide conventions and training events, however, our focus was on pastors' wives and others from around our state.

WARNING: BEING A FRIEND DOESN'T MEAN BEING GOSSIP PARTNERS

Friendship's purpose is not to provide a gossip partner. When you preface gossip with "We need to pray about this," it's still gossip. If you're the one listening when someone else gossips, it's still gossip. It's gossip if you're talking to the deacon chairman's wife about the church down the street or critiquing a staff member. If someone hopes to find out the inside scoop about church details or problems when you are vulnerable, then she's not the friend for you. If she shares gossip or negativity with you, hoping you'll pass it on to your spouse, you need a different friend.

Gossip's domino effect in the church is debilitating. Maybe that's why God's Word condemns gossip and slander so harshly. Have precious friends at church, but never gossip with them.

"You must have your own personal prayer warriors, not from your congregation. They should be godly ladies you trust and who are honest with you. Your church family does love you, but they struggle with you having sin, family problems, etc., like they do."

—EILEEN SHEETS (MRS. JIM), RIFLE, CO

WARNING: BEING A FRIEND DOESN'T MEAN "DUMPING"

Have you ever been betrayed by someone in whom you've confided? It's the same story I've heard over and over from ministers' wives, and it can destroy her ministry and her husband's. This warning is written in flashing red lights. When burdens are heavy and you need a confidante, she should probably not be a congregation member.

There is a fine line between being open with a dear friend, and sharing inappropriately with church members. A minister's wife should *never* confide her marital problems or negative feelings about church issues to a friend who is a church member. She is often privy to private details about church matters and members' personal lives, but those should never be confided to a friend. She may have negative opinions about something happening within the church, but she never rants or "dumps" those on her friend. Why?

When you "share" with a friend about your marital issue, you've likely negated your husband's ability to preach and minister to that person effectively. When a ministry wife speaks inappropriately with a friend who is a church member, it can crumble her husband's ministry. If you relay private church information, your reputation will be damaged, and your husband's trust in you will be hurt.

Andy Griggs sings a country song titled "This Ain't No Practice Life." Whether you're a 19-year-old youth ministry wife or an experienced senior pastor's wife, the truth is the same. There are no do-overs. Your actions and words can't be undone. Never allow your lips to betray your husband, your church, and your own ministry under the guise of friendship. Have precious friends, but without gossip or inappropriate conversations.

The heart of the Proverbs 31 woman's husband trusted her completely (v. 11). If you—even once!—share private or inappropriate information with a friend, your husband will lose that important trust in you.

A friend can betray you, disappoint you, or even turn on you. It happened to Jesus. It happened to Paul. Don't avoid having friends, however. A worthy confidante is a treasure for a ministry wife.

> *It is not an enemy who taunts me—I could bear that. It is not my foes who so arrogantly insult me—I could have hidden from them. Instead, it is you—my equal, my companion and close friend. What good fellowship we once enjoyed as we walked together to the house of God.*
> PSALM 55:12–14

"Trust no one."

—A TONGUE-IN-CHEEK QUOTE FROM AN ANONYMOUS MINISTRY WIFE WHO REGRETTED HER OWN INAPPROPRIATE WORDS

"Find a woman you trust—a pastor's wife or older friend who loves you and your family very much, but isn't connected to your church— to turn to for prayer, support, encouragement. Those friendships have countless value."
—AMY COOPER, MARSHAL, IL

WHEN YOU NEED A CONFIDANTE

If a ministry wife can't confide church problems and personal dilemmas with girlfriends from church, where can she find a confidante? From my personal experience, and in observing many ministry wives, here are four suggestions:

Talk to God, your intimate best friend, the One who "sees you" (Genesis 16:13). He gets you. He's always available. Always wise. Always loving. His comfort is life changing. His resources are unlimited. Jesus calls us His friend (John 15:12–17). Talk to Him. He cares more about your church or problem than you! "Pour out your heart to Him, for God is our refuge" (Psalm 62:8).

106

Talk to your minister-husband. My husband is my best friend on earth. He's a wonderful confidante, and he truly cares about me and the things on my mind. He hurts when I hurt. And he's got great wisdom.

Find a Christian friend outside your church ministry area. Carefully consider a wise, godly, older woman, a faithful friend, who is not part of your local church or ministry. She may be a longtime friend, a trusted ministry wife, or someone you served with in a previous church. If you feel absolutely confident in her, find a way to spend time together, and share your heart. Seek her wisdom. Ask her to pray with you. I've had several such valuable confidantes in my life. In retrospect, I believe their calm, listening ear was healing, and their outside perspective helped lead to wise decisions.

If your burdens are extreme, find professional Christian counseling. Many retreat settings, staffed by professional Christian counselors are designed specifically for ministry couples.

FAMILY VERSUS MINISTRY

There's a new fallacy floating around ministry conferences these days. I sat in a large class for church planters' wives recently where the speaker loudly ranted about pastors who are too invested in ministry. She adamantly instructed young wives to put their foot down hard, and tell their minister-husbands they can only do ministry on two nights per week. (Foot stomp) Period. (Foot stomp) No exceptions. (Foot stomp).

She told them to make their husbands turn off the phone, don't answer the door, and don't even think about responding to someone else's emergency. He shouldn't counsel, do church meetings, fellowship, revivals, or events on those evenings. His family needs his evening hours, she said.

We've all read blogs and books declaring war between the pastoral family and the church. It sounds noble at first, yet there is no war between God, His mission, and your family. God gave you that family!

Your family is enormously important, and a strategic part of your ministry itself. A minister and his wife, however, can both serve in a church *and* rear balanced, happy children. Yes, it's a constant effort to balance life. First Timothy 3:4–5 instructs a minister to manage his own family well, having children who respect and obey him. His involvement and investment in his children is absolutely vital. Deuteronomy instructs parents to disciple children "as they go." But that doesn't mean ministry stops at 5:00 p.m.

My minister-husband loves his job and pours his life into ministry. He also adores his wife and family. Although we served in growing, active churches while rearing our kids, we found his flexible work schedule actually allowed him to be more involved in their lives than many parents. He hardly ever missed a ball game or major event. If he had evening meetings, he'd make a point to be at home another time during the day. Some weeks are harder than others, but a minister can be both a wonderful minister and a fabulous husband and dad.

I believe that speaker was trying to impress the importance of spending quality time as a family, but instead, some of those wives came away with the empowerment to "put their foot down" and tell their man when he can serve God and when he can't. Building barriers is not ministry. That foot-stomping demand being taught to pastors' wives had three flaws.

First flaw: It was a foot-stomping demand. The Bible instructs wives to respect their husband and follow his leadership. There should be no foot-stomping, my-way-or-the-highway tantrum.

Second flaw: It is unreasonable. A church's worship, small groups, meetings, outreach events, community ministries, weddings, fellowships, counseling—practically everything is scheduled for evenings or weekends so most people who work can participate.

Crises that demand immediate ministry, such as death, fire, or natural disasters can occur any time, day or night.

Third flaw: Resentment doesn't look good on you. When a minister is busy doing his God-called work, but his wife is angry and bitter, her attitude overflows onto the children. Proverbs 25:24 reads, "It's better to live alone in the corner of an attic than with a quarrelsome wife in a lovely home." We can have personal family time without building rigid walls.

Ministry can be challenging, demanding, and time-consuming, but our family should be a beneficiary, not a victim. Don't declare a family versus church war. Be a family who loves serving God. Our commitment is to be a wise and joyful servant of God. Without stomping feet.

We the couple.

We the family.

We the church.

"We" takes the load off of "I." It truly simplifies a ministry wife's life. Will you take the "we" challenge? For the next two weeks, make a conscientious effort to say and demonstrate the word *we* in all three areas of your life. Say "we."

NEXT STEP
TAKE ACTION
A LOOK AT THE BOOK
SIMPLE FRESH IDEAS   **MY COMMITMENT TO GOD**

❏ I will be a positive partner in ministry with my husband.

❏ I will help my children have joy as PKs.

❏ I will help my children discover and use their spiritual gifts.

❏ I will be intentional about teaching our children about God through my words and life.

❏ I will find at least one ministry involvement at church, and pour myself into it.

❑ I will be visibly a part of our church.

❑ I will say we the couple, we the family, and we the church.

❑ And I will put actions to those words.

NEXT STEP
TAKE ACTION
A LOOK AT THE BOOK
SIMPLE FRESH IDEAS

Pick some action activities to reinforce your study about "Simple Step #4: Say 'We.'"

❑ Work with your husband to write a brief family purpose statement based on Joshua 24:15. Frame it.

❑ Discuss your family purpose statement with the children.

❑ Do a Bible word study of *friend*. Use Proverbs 12:26; 13:20; 22:24–25; 27:17; and other Scriptures as a reference to write out a "WANT AD" for a friend.

❑ Memory verse: *"A worthy wife is a crown for her husband, but a disgraceful woman is like cancer in his bones." Proverbs 12:4*

❑ Chat with your husband about your church's perception of you as a married couple and you as a supportive ministry wife. Brainstorm ways to improve that perception.

❑ Consider these things to do together as a couple in ministry.

■ Specific thing I do to encourage my husband in ministry.

■ Something we've done to help our children feel part of the ministry team.

■ A great discipleship idea for parents.

■ Something I do to show I'm part of the body of Christ.

❑ A one-week challenge: Make a conscientious effort to say and demonstrate the word *we* in these three areas of your life: marriage, family, church family. Say "we."

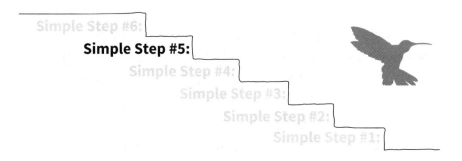

Simple Step #6:

Simple Step #5:

Simple Step #4:

Simple Step #3:

Simple Step #2:

Simple Step #1:

Be Resilient

But the Holy Spirit produces this kind of fruit in our lives: . . . peace, patience, . . . gentleness, and self-control. GALATIANS 5:22–23

*Y*ou can see nothing but water wildly splashing in every direction. The guy is flailing and choking and screaming, going under water, then miraculously coming up for another gasp of air. It's a horrific drowning incident, until someone from the shore yells, "Just stand up!!"

It's a scene from the movies, or a scene from real life, but it shouldn't be a scene in our Christian life. There will be trials and troubles in life and in ministry. Plan ahead for your response. Our loving Savior promises to see us through anything that comes our way. He doesn't want us to flail around. He wants us to stand on His foundation.

Here on earth you will have many trials and sorrows. But take heart, because I have overcome the world.
JOHN 16:33

"My suffering is bigger than your suffering" can become an anthem when ministry wives are together. Is your favorite song, "Nobody Knows the Trouble I've Seen"? Any ministry wife could relate saga after saga about troubles, in ministry, maybe even life-threatening persecution from inside or outside the church.

My husband is not an overly emotional guy, but there were tears in his eyes this morning as he finished the phone call from a pastor in another state. In that pastor's decade-long tenure, the church has grown, built a new building, and developed a great reputation for community ministry and evangelism in their community. This morning, the deacons walked into the pastor's office and gave him an envelope, asking him to read it after they left. They had learned that another church had the pastor's résumé, and they were furious. The letter instructed him to resign immediately, effective this Saturday, and not return on Sunday. Devastation!

Yes, there are some true horror stories. When small or large problems arise in ministry, our responsibility is to handle them in a way that does not dishonor the God who saved you. Study 2 Corinthians 6:1–10.

When any type of trouble arises, we must make a choice. When we're surrounded, will we fight and gasp and struggle, even drown in those troubles? Or will we simply stand on God's foundation? Let's talk about how to honor God during those times.

"Hurt people hurt people. . . . But because of God's grace I can love the hurting."
—LYNETTE EZELL (MRS. KEVIN), MILTON, GA

When troubles come, God is bigger. Here are some tips to help your calm response.

BE RESILIENT

Be confident in God's call on your life. When you know you're in His will, you can bounce back when trouble comes. You're not just called to serve Him in good times. The test is in the hard days. "Fight the good fight for the true faith. Hold tightly to the eternal life to which God has called you" (1 Timothy 6:12).

I have known many ministry wives who have become bitter and angry—and even ended their husband's ministry—because they don't choose to get over things. Stand. Be resilient.

"This has worked in every situation for over 40 years of ministry—Psalm 62:5 reads, 'My soul, wait silently for God alone, for my expectation is from Him.'"
                                        —KK KAREN GILBERT (MRS. AL), ROSWELL, GA

Let God do the payback. Never take revenge. Never retaliate. Forgiveness means no payback. No scowls. No avoiding them. If they have hurt you personally, leave any retaliation to God.

> *Dear friends, never take revenge. Leave that to the righteous anger of God. For the Scriptures say, 'I will take revenge; I will pay them back,' says the LORD.*
> ROMANS 12:19–21.

"Love the church people, and don't get your feelings hurt easily. 'Love does not hold grudges and will hardly even notice when others do it wrong'" (1 Corinthians 13:5).
                                        —ELLA HOUVENAGLE (MRS. MARK), ROCKVILLE, IN

DON'T BE EASILY OFFENDED

This is a big one for a ministry wife! When someone says something untrue about us or hurts our feelings, we don't quit serving God.

Learn to let unkind words "slide off your back." My friend Dana James says, "Pray for holy 'Rain-X'—for the words to simply run off and not penetrate." Forgive. Again.

"Show compassion to your people, your husband, your children, and yourself. No one is perfect!"

—PAULA KELLERMEYER (MRS. CHRIS), PENDLETON, IN

Do the "heaping coals" trick.

> *If your enemies are hungry, give them food to eat. If they are thirsty, give them water to drink. You will heap burning coals of shame on their heads, and the LORD will reward you.* PROVERBS 25:21–23

Be kind to your enemies. There are some people—even in churches— whose behavior is simply mean. How shall we deal with naysayers, persecutors, gossipers, troublemakers, and unkind church members? "Love your enemies! Do good to those who hate you. Bless those who curse you. Pray for those who hurt you" (Luke 6:27–28). Love them publicly and privately. Love them sincerely. Love them in spite of their unloveableness. Be kind to them.

> *For you [God] are my hiding place; you protect me from trouble. You surround me with songs of victory.* PSALM 32:7

REMEMBER WHO'S REALLY IN CHARGE

Handling fear begins with trusting God on the front end, and He will handle our fear. "Don't be afraid . . . for you are very precious to God. Peace! Be encouraged! Be strong!" (Daniel 10:19). Read His Word daily, and He will comfort you through it. God promises peace. Don't live in a constant state of drama or panic. Rest in God. Repeat these words: "I trust in God so why should I be afraid? What can mere mortals to do me?" (Psalm 56:11).

> *I will trust in Him and not be afraid.*   Isaiah 12:2

Hug your husband on difficult days. Lean on him. Pull closer together as a couple.

> *Two people are better off than one, for they can help each other succeed. If one person falls, the other can reach out and help.*   Ecclesiastes 4:9–10

"To be chosen to partner with one of God's select servants is a huge honor. Never forget that, particularly in the hard times."

—CINDY EVERS (MRS. FRED), TIFTON, GA

Tattle to your Father. Run to God! Get on your knees and pour out your troubles. Ask Him for wisdom and strength. Trust Him totally. He's never failed you yet, and He cares deeply. Read Psalm 36:5–10 aloud. Twice.

> *Give all your worries and cares to God, for he cares about you.*   1 Peter 5:7

STAY NEAR THE IRON

Proverbs 27:17 says that a friend sharpens a friend like iron sharpens iron. Have you ever heard of the 90/10 rule? I read about it in a business magazine years ago, but the principle fits here. Make a point to spend at least 90 percent of your church ministry with positive church members, and 10 percent or less with the negative ones. It's tempting to focus all our efforts on the "squeaky wheel" folks—those who are complaining, overly negative, troublemakers—who probably won't ever be happy anyway. One pastor's wife explained it this way: "I feel like I'm being nibbled to death by ducks!" One little peck isn't bad, but when it's constant, difficult people can consume you. Yes, we love them and definitely minister to them. But when we concentrate the majority of our ministry time with church members who share our heart for Jesus, they bring us up, and we can all accomplish God's Great Commission better.

OPEN YOUR LOVE NOTES FILE

I begin a new folder each year, labeled *Love Notes*. You could call it your rainy day folder. My friend Cindy Traylor labels hers *Happy File*, and she says it's kept her going on more than one occasion! In that simple manila folder, stash encouraging notes you receive. A compliment from an email. A note from a grieving widow. A crayon note from a child. When days are difficult in ministry, a quick glance in the folder reminds me of my purpose and reignites my commitment. It's almost as if God is saying, "Keep on!"

"Contentment is both commended (godliness with contentment is great gain) and commanded (be content with what you have) . . . but what a hard discipline."

—LAUREN MILLICAN (MRS. NATHAN), JEFFERSONVILLE, IN

DRESS APPROPRIATELY

Just for fun, picture this. You're going into a horrendous battlefield, and you're wearing a T-shirt, shorts, and flip-flops. You're terrified as you step into a sea of bullets zinging around you.

Second scenario: You're going into a horrendous battlefield, but you're wearing a full-body bulletproof Kevlar outfit. Your ultimate safety is totally assured.

Scripture describes our everyday life as a battle. The devil's snares are all around us. As Christians, we can choose to walk into the battle naked—on our own power, with no protection, or we can choose to wear the bulletproof armor of God that He supplies. It's better than Kevlar, and it's only available to God followers who choose daily to wear it. Don't fight battles without His armor. Before heading to the battlefield today, get yours here: Ephesians 6:10–18. As you read these verses, visualize how you'll wear each piece of God's armor.

LEARN SOMETHING

It's amazing how much you can learn during difficult days. You learn to lean on God in ways you've never done before. When you've personally experienced any hurt, you will be able to minister to hurting people in a deeper way. For example, when someone criticizes, ask yourself if there could be a small truthful element in the criticism. If you handle it calmly, you may learn and improve. You may even learn to appreciate constructive criticism.

BE CONTENT AND JOYFUL

Especially in difficult times. The psalmist declared that all who take refuge in Him are happy (Psalm 2:12). James told believers that when troubles come, they should consider it an opportunity for great joy. Keep a sense of humor. When others see your joy during challenges, there is no doubt who you serve!

KEEP YOUR EYES ON THE PRIZE

When handling difficult people and circumstances, contemplate eternity. Paul said, "I press on to reach the end of the race and receive the heavenly prize for which God, through Christ Jesus, is calling us" (Philippians 3:14). Remember that there are rewards awaiting you! One of the most eye-opening and motivating books I've ever read is *This*

Was Your Life by Jamie Lash and Rick Howard. It's an entire book about rewards in heaven. It would encourage any ministry wife.

It was the 25th anniversary celebration for University Baptist Church in San Antonio. We had served as church planters there for almost seven years during its infancy (when church planting wasn't cool!). We began with nine people, counting children, meeting in a school cafeteria. We did the usual planting tasks—hauling equipment, serving the community, clearing land, building buildings. It had been slow, laborious, thrilling work, and every year God blessed the new church with many new Christians and numeric growth. When we left, the church had grown to several hundred, and it is still a vibrant, evangelistic body of believers.

We could hardly wait for the big anniversary celebration, and what a day! It felt like a small taste of what heaven may hold. Children in that church plant had grown into strong, God-loving adults. They were now real adults serving God across the globe—a seminary professor, a state congressman, leaders of all kinds in their churches and communities. People we'd introduced to Jesus were now leading ministries in the church. Many young people from beginning days now brought their children and grandchildren. It was a heritage of faith. When you're enduring hardships in ministry life, you rarely think of future children and grandchildren and churches who will be impacted for all eternity because of your work today. Keep your eyes on the prize.

Remember, too, God's church is His loved bride. If God moves you to serve in a different church or ministry, be sure no one leaves your former church because of you. Be very cautious with parting words. Like Paul in Acts 15:41, leave the church stronger because of your time there.

Work willingly at whatever you do, as though you were working for the Lord rather than for people.

Remember that the Lord will give you an inheritance as your reward, and that the Master you are serving is Christ.　　　Colossians 3:23–24

FORGIVE. AGAIN.

"Forgive. Whether it's our husband, friend, or someone from ministry, we must forgive because of the great forgiveness our Lord gave us. If you want to have a fruitful ministry, you must be forgiving."

—JENNIFER, LEON, GUANAJUATO

YOUR CHOICE: WANT TO WEAR A CROWN OF BEAUTY OR DIRTY ASHES?

Isaiah 61:1–3. When trouble comes, God doesn't want His children to sit around moping in despair. Take a look at this Scripture:

The spirit of the Sovereign Lord is upon me, for the Lord has anointed me to bring good news to the poor. He has sent me to comfort the brokenhearted and to proclaim that captives will be released and prisoners will be freed. He has sent me to tell those who mourn that the time of the Lord's favor has come, and with it, the day of God's anger against their enemies. To all who mourn in Israel, He will give a crown of beauty for ashes, a joyous blessing instead of mourning, festive praise instead of despair. In their righteousness, they will be like great oaks that the Lord has planted for his own glory.　　　Isaiah 61:1–3

In biblical times, ashes symbolized grief and mourning. A swipe of ash was placed on one's forehead to indicate inner hurt. We get a similar picture in the classic fairy tale, when Cinderella is sitting by the fireplace, covered in ashes. She's sad and mourning her own miserable state of affairs.

God's comfort in trouble, however, is much better than a romantic fairy tale. God takes us, in real-life circumstances, and trades those ashes for a crown of beauty. He trades grief for joy. Festive oil instead of mourning. A garment of praise instead of despair. Wow!

God doesn't promise we'll never have trouble or trials or sorrow. But He does promise to be with us through those times. Psalm 23 and Psalm 91 are lovely pictures of God's comfort in trouble. As "oaks of righteousness," our roots are deep in God. We can stand tall in troubled times.

Don't mope in the ashes of life difficulties. Look up to God. He'll exchange your sad ashes for a crown of beauty.

What should I do when I've had it up to here?

Close your mouth. Change your facial expression. Blink, then look at the person through God's loving eyes.

Pause. Take a long slow breath. Do not respond quickly. Sometimes a pause is all it takes to calm the situation. Sometimes no response is required at all.

During that pause, send up a "shotgun prayer." Prayer changes things. Know God can handle any problem. Ask Him to give you wisdom, and to speak through you.

Speak His name, Jesus. Even spoken inaudibly, it can calm you down.

Respond slowly, in a peaceful, quiet, kind voice.

Burn coals, not bridges. No matter the circumstance, show love.

Never exude a bad attitude or snarky disposition. Even if you're right, don't be cocky. Silently quote the "fruit of the Spirit" attributes, if that helps!

If you're about to cry and really want to stop the tears, press your finger hard on your philtrum, the indention between your nose and upper lip. It works.

Remember this: If you misbehave right now, it makes the offender look good, and may negate any future ministry to them.

Start break dancing. That will throw the other person off for sure. (OK, I'm kidding on this one, but just the thought may help change your face.)

> *You have turned my mourning into joyful dancing.*
> *You have taken away my clothes of mourning and*
> *clothed me with joy.*   PSALM 30:11

Some things we consider suffering are actually just results from our own sin. Do your best to live a life that honors your God every moment. I read a tweet from Rick Warren: "God gave us mouths that close and ears that don't. What does that tell us? 'You must all be quick to listen, slow to speak, and slow to get angry' (James 1:19). If you do the first two, the third is automatic."

Some things we think of as suffering are actually real ministry opportunities. They may be inconvenient, but God uses "all things to the good" for those who love Him.

Steve was a bivocational pastor during seminary years. Every Friday after work and school, we'd drive an hour to our tiny church, Valley Creek Baptist, just outside Leonard, a small rural town in Texas. We'd work voraciously, and return for work and school early Monday morning. We slept on a roller-coaster-shaped sleeper sofa in a parsonage room built on the back of the church. We listened to wolves howl and critters thump under the building at night. Our paycheck didn't cover the gas cost. There was no phone, and we burned our own trash. We actually ate squirrel stew at a deacon's home, and rang the huge bell on Sunday mornings. Were we "suffering for Jesus"?

Quite the contrary! We were serving Jesus just as He called. We were learning to love people and gaining invaluable experiences. Steve was getting to preach. We were thankful to God to have a place to serve, and threw ourselves into ministering there.

God never promised ministry would be easy; in fact, He warned that trouble will come. And He promises to be with you when it does. Remember God's call on your life. Be resilient. Don't flop or sputter or flail or drown. Just stand up. Stand on His firm foundation.

NEXT STEP
TAKE ACTION
A LOOK AT THE BOOK
SIMPLE FRESH IDEAS **MY COMMITMENT TO GOD**

❑ I will remember God's faithfulness in the past.

❑ I will let God give any payback when someone wrongs me.

❑ I will forgive.

❑ I will try the "holy Rain-X" approach when someone speaks wrongly about me.

❑ I will be kind to my enemies.

❑ I will remember that God is in control. Not them. Not me.

❑ I will forgive.

❑ I will spend more ministry time with positive people than negative.

❑ I will learn contentment from Paul.

❑ I will keep my eyes on the prize.

❑ I will forgive. Again.

NEXT STEP

TAKE ACTION

A LOOK AT THE BOOK

SIMPLE FRESH IDEAS **STRESS BUSTERS**

Pick a couple of these stress-buster action activities to reinforce what your study of "Simple Step #5: Be Resilient."

❑ Do a Bible word study on *forgiveness*.

❑ Keep remembering the call of God on your life.

❑ Take an hourlong stroll, and pour out your heart to God.

❑ If someone really gets on your nerves, read Matthew 18:22. Now use your Notes app or a notecard to add a mark each time you forgive him or her. Keep an ongoing tab until you reach 490 marks. That's 70 times 7. (I know that verse means forgive without limit, but keeping marks might help.)

❑ Study 2 Corinthians 6:1–10. Look for nine conditions (hardships) to endure (vv. 4–5), nine characteristics to exhibit during hardship (vv. 6–7), and nine contrasts to embrace (vv. 8–10). That was my pastor's sermon outline this week—thanks, Pastor Ted Traylor.

❑ Begin and end the day affirming your complete trust in God. Before your head leaves the pillow in the night, before your toes touch the floor in the morning, talk to Him.

❑ Memory challenge: Watch for a little glass or ceramic pig you can place near your kitchen sink. Now memorize this verse, and quote it every time you notice that pig: "A beautiful woman who lacks discretion is like a gold ring in a pig's snout" (Proverbs 11:22).

❑ Listen to your favorite Christian music.

❑ Read one chapter in Psalms. Out loud.

❑ Play outside with a child for an hour. If you don't have a child, borrow one.

❑ Take the first item on your to-do list, and do it very well. Right now.

❑ Take a bubble bath, and sing a favorite praise song out loud. Even if you don't sing well.

❑ Make a list of at least ten very specific things you're thankful for.

❑ Call someone who's hurting and invite them to meet for lunch.

❑ Read Habakkuk 3:17.

❑ Search your Bible for an appropriate Scripture for today. Print and tape it to your mirror or computer screen.

❑ Chat with your husband about the problem for less than five minutes, then ask him to pray for you about it.

❑ *Discuss these questions with a ministry wife friend:

   ◾ How do you combat loneliness?

   ◾ How do you stay "up" when you're husband is down?

   ◾ What's your secret for contentment?

   ◾ Have you ever done something nice for a troublemaker?

NEXT STEP
TAKE ACTION
A LOOK AT THE BOOK
SIMPLE FRESH IDEAS **FOR CONQUERING LONELINESS**

It's an amazing phenomenon. A ministry wife may have church members constantly around her. She may be known throughout the city by name. She may be effective in ministry, successful professionally, admired and loved and busy with work she loves. Yet, she may feel great loneliness at times. I've gathered a few ideas that have helped me. Maybe one will pep you up on a lonely day.

◾ Read Psalm 143. Many Psalm writings are cry-out-to-God chapters that will touch your heart.

◾ Go to a coffee shop. Read a good book and sip tea.

- Call the most recent widow in your church, and take her to lunch. Listen and show God's love.
- Put on your running shoes and walk around the nearest gym or track. Talk to God as you walk.
- Be a local tourist and go see something you've not seen before.
- Make a list of God's blessings.
- Get a haircut or color. Hey—it works for me.
- Call a neighbor you've been meaning to introduce to Christ. Invite her for tea.
- Go sit in your church's worship center and pray.
- Call your husband, tell him you're coming to kidnap him for an hour, and feed ducks at the park together.
- Call a young mom you know and offer to babysit for an hour.
- Make friends with the wife of your associational strategist or state denominational executive (your denomination may use different terminology, but you get the idea).
- Call someone you love, and listen. Your mom. Or your daughter. Or your mentor.
- Enroll in a class.
- Call a single woman in your church and encourage her. Invite her for dinner with your family.
- Find somewhere in the community to volunteer once a week.

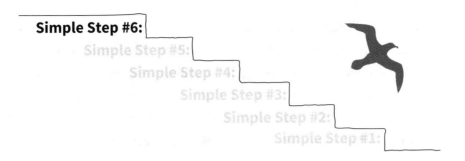

Simple Step #6:

Simple Step #5:

Simple Step #4:

Simple Step #3:

Simple Step #2:

Simple Step #1:

Serve Passionately

But the Holy Spirit produces this kind of fruit in our lives: . . . goodness, faithfulness. GALATIANS 5:22

"Seek and follow God's good and perfect path for you and be yourself, always!" —TERRY SCARBOROUGH (MRS. GARY), ASHTON, MD

Serve passionately. *That's not simple,* you're thinking. Oh, but it is! Read on.

Did you know a ministry wife could unintentionally hijack a church's effectiveness and growth by trying to do everything herself? Imagine a human body that looks exactly like one huge thumb. It's not a pretty sight, is it? It's not a functional or reasonable picture. When God's Word describes the church as the body of Christ, it states that each member of the church body has his or her own responsibility. God gave every Christian spiritual gifts, and those are to be used in the church body.

A church is not designed for one person or one couple to accomplish every function. A well-intentioned, but overfunctioning minister or ministry wife can rob others of joyful service to God! Ephesians 4:12

explains the pastor's responsibility is to "equip God's people to do His work and build up the church, the body of Christ." Equipping involves teaching, training, mentoring, and modeling. Rather than robbing others of ministry, help equip them and build up God's church. Oh, it's tempting to do it all. You're both excited and committed. You could probably do it all better by yourselves. But when you share the ministry load, you share the blessings.

Conversely, it's critical that a ministry wife intentionally discovers her spiritual gifts and plugs passionately into what God has called her to do in His church. Laziness in ministry does not honor God. Church members need to observe her working alongside them in ministry. Describing Pharisees, the religious leaders, Jesus said, "They crush people with unbearable religious demands and never lift a finger to ease the burden" (Matthew 23:4).

In summary: Don't do everything in the church; but what you do, do it with great passion.

"Realizing God made each of us special, use your God-given gifts and talents." —*Kay Towers (Mrs. Jimmy), Killeen, TX*

It was a huge change when God called Steve to serve as pastor in a struggling church. It was smaller than our previous church, and required a substantial salary adjustment. But more importantly, it was a downward-spiraling, desperate church with a harmed community reputation and horrific financial problems. We had no experience with those challenges. How could God trust us with such a task? But we knew it was His call, and moved our three children and our hearts to this new missions field.

As we prayed, Steve and I determined we would serve God with all we could give—with passion—and we would pour our lives into helping restore joy to His church. I jumped into helping with fifth-grade Sunday

School and bringing the women joyfully together. I'd never served in either ministry area, but learned everything I could, and involved lots of people in helping with both ministries.

Five years later, our thriving youth ministry was fueled by incoming youth from the fifth-grade department, consistently the largest class in the church. Our women's ministry focused on missions, ministry, and Christian growth, and, surprisingly, had grown into one of the largest and most outward-focused in our entire state. It was a great turnaround church, with hearts changed and evangelism reignited. Our children were loved and growing in the Lord, and the church had exploded in growth.

What had appeared to be a suffering-for-Jesus kind of move had evolved into some of our most fruitful years of ministry. We were serving passionately, exactly where God called us. Difficult? Absolutely. But seeing God begin a new work in His church made it worthwhile. That church today is still a bright light for Christ in that major American city.

Will you find your ministry and serve with passion? You don't have to play the piano or teach the women's Bible class. Serve where God directs you, and do it with great passion.

How to Find Your Ministry in Church

So how does a ministry wife find her place of ministry in her church?

If you're already serving in God's church exactly where He's placed you, keep on! Remember God has gifted you differently than others who are reading this. Consider your personality and energy level. You may enjoy serving in one ministry or several, but when you're doing what God has called you to do, you can do it with great passion.

"Don't worry about what 'everyone else' expects you to be as the pastor's wife; focus on who God calls you to be and you'll find contentment." —SHELIA GUSTAFSON (MRS. CHRIS), JEFFERSONVILLE, IN

Here are six tips to help discern where God wants you to serve in the church body:

1. Talk to God about it. Pray to your Father in heaven. Ask His guidance as you consider how to serve. He may inspire you to change ministries at different stages of life, and that's fine. For example, when our third baby was born, I took a year sabbatical from the teen's Bible class I loved to teach. Instead, I served as a much-needed greeter at the welcome desk, and spent Sunday afternoons calling first-time church guests. God provided a different ministry that worked with my parenting schedule.

Diligently seek God's guidance. As you pray, observe needs in your church. As you read the Sunday worship program, God may prick your heart about an opportunity. If you're hesitant to commit, volunteer as a substitute in some area of ministry while you pray.

> *And so I tell you, keep on asking, and you will receive what you ask for. Keep on seeking, and you will find. Keep on knocking, and the door will be opened to you.* Luke 11:9

"When I realized that each woman in our first church had a different expectation of me, I got on my knees and asked God to help me to live my life to please Him! This has given me peace, and freedom to serve Him with joy." —KAREN LIEVERS (MRS. RUSS), CLARKSVILLE, IN

2. Discover your spiritual gifts. If you know exactly how God has gifted you, write your spiritual gifts on this page's margin. If you're somewhat uncertain, study 1 Peter 4:10–11, 1 Corinthians 12, Ephesians 4, and Romans 12 afresh. Ask God for discernment to know what gifts He's given you. Then diligently watch for ways you can use them in the church. Once you've determined how God has gifted you to serve Him in the church, everything is filtered through that sieve. There will probably be times you'll help to serve in other areas, but if you've determined God's calling, it's simpler to say yes when the opportunity arises.

> *God has given each of you a gift from his great variety of spiritual gifts. Use them well to serve one another.* 1 PETER 4:10

"Your spiritual gifts help you define where you are most effective as a partner in ministry." —JODI CHAPMAN (MRS. MORRIS), FRANKLIN, TN

3. **Talk with your husband.** He knows you and your gifts and interests. He knows the church, and may have wisdom or suggestions about where you may serve most effectively. As you enjoy the partnership in ministry with your husband, talk often with him about ways you can minister with him and separately from him in the church. Ask his opinion and wisdom about your gifts and talents.

> *Plans succeed through good counsel.* PROVERBS 20:18

4. **Talk with a mature Christian woman you respect, who knows your strengths.** This could be a mentor, a friend from a previous church, or someone in your church. Brainstorm about ministries you might enjoy, and listen to her wisdom and prayer. Talk with the staff person or volunteer in charge of a potential area of ministry you're considering. Yes, you are the minister's wife, but that means it's even more important that you observe proper channels. Don't abuse your connection with the pastor to bypass the education minister or other person in charge. Make an appointment. Ask strategic questions.

Meet co-workers. Observe needs and potential.

> *So anyone one who rebels against authority is rebel-*
> *ling against what God has instituted.*   Romans 13:2

5. **Say yes with delight.** When you determine God is leading, say yes wholeheartedly. Don't behave as if you're doing someone a favor.

I hadn't been a pastor's wife too long when an older ministry wife pulled me aside. "They can't make you do one thing in this church. You're not on the payroll!" she advised. I thought long and hard about that comment. A ministry wife, and any Christian, serves God simply because she loves Him. She doesn't need to be coerced into serving.

A popular breakout class for ministers' wives conferences is often titled something like "How to Say No" or "Just Say No!" Be careful of your noes. Pray first, then if it's not something God inspires, gently and confidently decline. If possible, help find someone else who would enjoy that project. My goal is to say yes every time God will lead and allow. Then when I need to say, "No, thank you," I can do it with confidence too.

> *Pay attention to the ministry you have received in*
> *the Lord, so that you can accomplish it.*
> Colossians 4:17 (HCSB)

If you're inclined to overcommit at church, read this ministry wife's experience:

"I tend to jump in with both feet in everything I do. It took me way too long to learn to say, 'Let me pray about that and I'll let you know next week. If the good Lord approves, I'm your girl!' That's still really hard

for me, because I'm a natural doer. However, it allows me to accept the task only when 'the Boss' approves. Makes life a whole lot easier."

—RENA COOMER, HOPE, IN

I can empathize with Rena. I am happiest when I'm involved in multiple ministry areas. I have to listen carefully to God for direction. It's unlikely God would lead you to overcommit so much that your family doesn't have dinner or you don't get sleep! A mentor of mine used to say, "I'd rather burn out than rust out!" It's interesting, though, that when I'm busy with what God desires for my life, I feel energized rather than burned out.

But here's where the "simple" part comes in. Once you know how God has gifted you, and you know He's called you to be involved in a specific church ministry, there's great, great joy in serving. Serving God within your spiritual giftedness is hard work, but never a burden. What could have been a burden is now a delight. You're confident to say yes or no because you lean on God for direction.

> *So let's not get tired of doing what is good. At just the right time we will reap a harvest of blessing if we don't give up.* GALATIANS 6:9

"I've never played the piano, led women's group or VBS, but I help when I'm needed, I love the people, and I support my husband and his ministry. God has blessed me beyond measure."

—RAECHELLE HARLESS (MRS. CLARK), PLYMOUTH, IN

I love seeing the many ways ministers' wives serve. It's almost a guarantee your ministry will be quite different than the former minister's wife! I know an awesome pastor's wife who plays drums in the praise band and another who leads worship. One ministry wife actually cooks and serves Wednesday evening dinners to a very large crowd at her church weekly. And she truly loves it! Another organizes church sports. Some clean the church building, serve in the church media library, help with baptism, decision counseling, graphic arts, or marketing. They serve in every part of small groups or Sunday School. They may work in the sound booth, the church office, or the welcome center. One may direct the entire Vacation Bible School; another may serve cookies there. My pastor's wife, Liz, often prepares homemade unleavened bread for the Lord's Supper service. Each uses her God-given talents and spiritual gifts to serve Him.

Be flexible. When we moved to a new church years later, God led me to an age group I'd never considered. The church had few young adults, so we began a "nearlywed" class for engaged couples. Gathering a great team of mentors for them, we were prepared when God brought many couples—even several who didn't know God—for the class. If the ministry where you currently serve is self-sufficient, or if it's become stagnant, perhaps God is leading you to serve Him in a different capacity. Listen.

"Pray, observe where God can use your gifts and talents, then hold your head high and plug in. Excite and ignite others around you, and watch how God blesses the work of your hands!"

—KRISTI BEAN (MRS. DONALD), NEDERLAND, TX

SIMPLE FRESH IDEAS PASSION POINTERS

Try these easy ways to add passion to your current activity in ministry.

- Plan well. Plan consistently. Time spent in planning for your ministry project will probably save you time later.
- Plan ahead. By working ahead, your creativity will soar.

- Learn names of those you minister with and those to whom you minister.
- Work hard. Commit time and effort to pour yourself into doing that ministry "as unto the Lord!"
- Be creative. Add new elements often. Pray for God to give you fresh ideas to enhance that ministry.
- Open your wallet. There may not be a line item in the church budget for the ministry God has assigned you. If you need to spend a few dollars of your own, do it gladly.
- Smile when you serve. See chapter 2's "Look at the Book" study.
- Give your very best. Don't settle for mediocre if it's being done for God.
- Involve others. Invite friends to help when it's appropriate.
- Constantly be looking and thinking about ways to improve that ministry.
- Build a prayer network. Ask a few prayer warriors to lift that ministry in prayer faithfully.
- Add enthusiasm. Review Ephesians 6:7.

Serve Wholeheartedly

When you're serving God, give it all you've got!

Passion for your house has consumed me.

PSALM 69:9

Work hard to learn everything about your specific ministry. Read every book and website you can get your hands on. Take every class on the topic offered by your denomination. Find someone in a neighboring church who serves in a similar ministry, take her to lunch and learn. Become an expert.

Whatever you do, do it enthusiastically, as some-
thing done for the Lord and not for men.

COLOSSIANS 3:23 (HCSB)

Serve wholeheartedly, whether your task is small or large, behind the scenes or highly visible. If you're passing out worship programs at the door, rocking babies in the nursery, updating the church website, or anything else, do it very well.

For example, if you do the records for the third-grade children's Bible class before you go to your own class on Sundays, do it with gusto. Be in your place before the first child arrives. Bring a rose from your garden for the sign-in table. Learn every child's name. Keep notes so you can call a newcomer by name on his or her second visit. Welcome them as if they're important to God (they are, of course!) Notice if the child attends church alone or which parents belong to them. You could send a note or email if the child is absent, or prepare a small Christmas gift for each person. Go beyond expectations for your ministry. Whatever God has called you to do, do it with passion.

"When it comes to involvement in the church, do that one thing God has gifted you within your Christian walk, and do it mightily unto the Lord." —BETTY LAWLEY (MRS. JEFF), REMINGTON, IN

Another example. A ministry wife serves as a greeter at her church's welcome desk. She serves with passion. After completing their guest card, she escorts each family member to his or her classroom and takes the time to connect him or her with someone there so they're comfortable. She's personable, and shows genuine interest in each guest. She watches for them in worship, and may sit near them. She gets their contact information before she leaves worship, and sends a follow-up email or makes a phone call to see if they have further questions. She keeps a notebook so she'll be able to call them by name when they arrive next week. She does her ministry with passion.

Simply find where God wants you to serve Him, and give it your best effort.

> *So fear the* LORD *and serve him wholeheartedly.*
>
> JOSHUA 24:14

Only You

"Leave room in your schedule for the specific 'God-called' tasks that only you can do." —RENA COOMER (MRS. DAN), COLUMBUS, IN

I sat beside an attractive, middle-aged woman in church recently, and she proceeded to tell me about a note her pastor's wife had written to her. There was no particular reason for the correspondence. It was simply an encouragement note. I was intrigued that she would tell me—a total stranger—about it. I asked, "When did you receive this note?" "Oh," she said, "it was probably about a year ago."

The pastor's wife later told me about her note writing. She pens a snail mail or email note every day during daily devotional time with God. It might be to someone who sang or was baptized on Sunday, or someone with a specific need. On some days, she'll write an encouraging note to a church member, using the church directory as a checklist.

I learned a lot about a pastor's wife's influence that day. Even something as simple as a friendly note might have a significant impact on a church member. I had never realized the heavy impact of a pastor's wife's touch. As you say yes to serving in your church, be intentional to leave some time to accomplish some privileged ministries that only the ministry wife can do. For example:

■ Only you can hold the pastor's hand after church.

- Only you can minister to a grieving widow as her pastor's wife.
- Only you can offer a pastor's wife's prayer for a weeping woman in the ladies room.
- Only you can go home with the pastor at the end of the day.
- Only you can represent your church as "the pastor's wife" around your town.
- Only you can minister as the minister's wife. Your touch, prayer, phone call, banana pudding, or other small kindness is meaningful.
- Only you can mentor an entire church. Well, sort of. People often observe your response to blessings and crisis, your posture, parenting, clothing style, attitude, etc. Be aware of your silent influence.
- Only you can invite someone to the minister's home. As you eagerly "pursue hospitality" (Romans 12:13), relationships deepen.
- Only you can say, "The pastor and I want to welcome you to our church," as an introduction to the women's luncheon. Yes, you'll be called on occasionally to offer a greeting at the ladies event, or a testimony for the senior ladies class. If your knees knock at the mere thought of saying a few words in public, plan ahead now. Let's talk about that privilege.

Steve was the guest speaker at a vibrant church in our city. I was seated in the rear center section, enjoying the awesome worship music, when a gentleman made an announcement. "And now, we'll hear a word from our preacher's wife!" *How cool*, I thought. I hadn't met the pastor's wife, and strained to see her through the crowd. Embarrassingly, it seemed she must have stepped out for a moment. After a few silent moments, I glanced at my husband onstage. He was nodding his head. Hmmm. The announcer repeated his sentence, and I suddenly understood. "And now, we'll hear a word from our preacher's wife." He meant me! And every eye in the room was looking at me. Terror!

Requests for you to share a testimony may not often be quite that dramatic, but know this: We must always be ready to give a word about what God is doing in our lives (1 Peter 3:15). You may share only a sentence, like I did in that shocking circumstance, but praising God is what Christians do.

Plan ahead. Write out your personal testimony. If you can share it in two minutes, you can always add details for a longer opportunity. Identify a favorite Scripture and prepare a devotional about it today. Write your key points on notecards and keep them in your car's glove compartment or on your cell phone. You never know when it might come in handy. This preparation will help you be willing and ready, even if you're not gifted at speaking. (See further tips below.)

I Have to Speak in Public?

SOME SIMPLE TIPS FOR THE TIMID MINISTRY WIFE

Yes, you'll occasionally be called upon to welcome the crowd for the women's luncheon or introduce a speaker. If you love to speak, you'll have opportunities to share a devotional or testimony. If you don't like to speak in public, try not to sweat it. Here are some tips for ministry wives who hate to speak in public.

- Make it short. No one will complain if your talk, prayer, or introduction is brief.
- Prepare well. Don't "wing it." Ask God to guide your preparation. Ask your husband's advice. He does this all the time!
- Use a sticky tab or ribbon to mark Scriptures you'll use. It's amazing how Genesis can disappear when you're fumbling at the front.
- Use index cards or an iPad for notes. Write only key words or thoughts on a few cards.
- Look your best. Manicure your nails, accessorize your outfit, polish your shoes. Dress with unquestionable modesty, and remember

that a skirt looks shorter on stage. You'll feel more confident if you look nice.

- Find a quiet place where you can pray alone beforehand.
- Once you arrive, forget about yourself. Concentrate on others.
- Learn to use a microphone. Hold it by your bottom lip and speak normally.
- As you walk to the microphone, take a deep breath, and smile.
- Whatever you do, don't say, "I hate to speak in public" or "I'm so nervous."
- Find one or two friendly faces in the group, make eye contact with them, and speak slowly.
- Use a prop. It gives you something to do with your hands and helps illustrate your point. I enjoy using PowerPoint because people look at the screen.
- Use illustrations well. Women love personal stories.
- Be humble. Direct the listener toward God.

Talking Is a Gift by Rhonda Kelley and Monica Rose Brennan is written specifically for Christian women in ministry, and should probably be "required" reading for every ministry wife. It gives detailed advice from experts about how to prepare a talk, give a testimony, use gestures, and more.

One last "only you" statement. When the pastor's wife takes a moment to personally welcome a guest at church, it means a lot to them. Be friendly and approachable at church. If you're intimidated about introducing yourself to strangers, try these tips:

TIPS FOR MEETING STRANGERS AND CHURCH GUESTS
- Make a great effort to speak to each guest.
- Approach the person confidently, with a smile.
- Welcome them sincerely.

- Learn his or her name.
- Introduce yourself briefly. If you're at church, don't hide the fact that you're the minister's wife. They would like to know that.
- If you think you've met before, say, "I think I've met you before."
- Ask a question. "Is this your first time worshipping here?" or "Are you new to town?"
- Listen carefully for a clue to help minister to that person.
- You don't have to talk long to make them feel truly welcome.
- Be observant. Try to find some way you could help them. Example: If they have a teen, introduce him or her to a friendly teen and invite them to this week's fellowship.
- Introduce them to someone with a common interest.
- Print personal cards, similar to business cards, with your name and email or phone. Those are perfect for connecting with newcomers.
- Repeat their name as you leave. Write it in a small notebook or phone app as soon as you can do it unobserved. At home, put it on a sticky note where you'll see it and learn it.

"I like to share new ministry ideas with my husband. I've learned it's best to write ideas in a notebook, plan and pray a bit, then share it when he's not working on a sermon!"

—IVETH VASQUEZ (MRS. GUSTAVO), SEYMOUR, IN

Above All Else, Tell the Good News

Don't miss the main point of serving God! We can do ministry inside the church and in the community, but our Great Commission is to share Jesus with lost people and disciple them. Have you gotten sidetracked with doing good things, but ignored the main thing?

Develop a reputation as a soul-winner. Sharing God's gift is surprisingly easy. Simply tell your Jesus story. I've heard it said, "I'll be a witness, and use words if necessary." The problem with that saying is that words *are* necessary! As you live for Christ, people will be drawn to your good works; but when you actually tell them what God has done, eternity changes. If you share Jesus, you will be a soul-winner.

The place where you serve may not be easy, but nothing revives a difficult church better than new life. Steve and I have never moved to pastor a growing church. Each was either a new church plant or a declining church. We never moved *away from* a declining church. How did that happen? We were personally committed to bringing lost people to God and to His church, and teaching other Christians to share their faith. When new birth happens, a church is revived.

Would you like to serve in a growing church? Do these two things: (1) Pour yourself totally into serving God where you are today and (2) Personally tell others the good news about salvation through Jesus Christ.

> *"The master was full of praise. 'Well done, my good and faithful servant. You have been faithful in handling this small amount, so now I will give you many more responsibilities. Let's celebrate together.'"*
>
> MATTHEW 25:21

Personally tell others the good news. Always be cultivating witnessing relationships. When you share your own God story often, you will see salvations and church growth happen. Don't be intimidated. People want to know how to become a Christian! Talk about God in casual conversation, and when He prompts you, ask if the hearer would like to have God's gift. Commit to share Him at least weekly, and keep a journal to list those people's names. You won't be serving in a stagnant church if you are telling lost people about Jesus regularly.

Those who are wise will shine as bright as the sky, and those who lead many to righteousness will shine like the stars forever. DANIEL 12:3

SIMPLIFIED EVANGELISM

LUKE 19:1–10. Let's take a lesson in evangelism from Jesus! Open your Bible to the story of Zacchaeus in Luke 19:1–10 and follow along.

Step 1: Get out. Walk outside your home. Go outside your church building. Love your Christian friends, but don't build a fortress and barricade the doors. God's instructions in Matthew 28:19–20 basically say, "Go everywhere; make disciples; I'll go with you!" When you love Jesus, and meet people who don't know Him, evangelism happens. Go.

Step 2: See them. Going is not enough without action. We must open our eyes and notice lost people. They're everywhere. The harvest is abundant (Matthew 9:37). And most lost people desperately want to get found. Zacchaeus ran. He climbed a tree, for goodness' sake! Lost people around you are leaning forward, watching as you shine for Christ. They're waiting for you to tell them about Him.

Step 3: Speak up. Jesus saw; He spoke. His words were personal. He called Zach by name, and even invited himself to Zach's house for a one-on-one conversation. God calls us His "letter." He warns us to always be ready to acknowledge Him and tell His good news (Matthew 10:32–33; 2 Corinthians 3:2–3; 1 Peter 3:15). How?

You can simply, conversationally tell how God saved you and how He makes a difference in your everyday life. You can mark the four verses and use the "Roman Road." You could download an effective witnessing conversation app called 3 Circles at namb.net. You can study William Fay's *Share Jesus Without Fear.* You can explain a witnessing bracelet or tract, or draw pictures, or bring the person to church with you. The key step is to open your mouth and tell what Jesus did for you. The method is not nearly as important as doing it! Initial here _____ if you will commit to share the plan of salvation with someone before next Friday.

Step 4: Watch results happen. Note: If you didn't initial above, reconsider. Then read on. If you share God's plan of salvation, people will respond. Zacchaeus welcomed Jesus joyfully. He believed. He was saved for all eternity. Many lives around him were impacted. You may not know the actual results until you get to heaven. If you don't see an immediate result, be aware God is at work.

Step 5: Expect complaints. There's a surprise ending. "All the people who saw it began to complain, 'He's gone to lodge with a sinful man'" (v. 6). Expect resistance. When lost people get saved, the angels in heaven are shouting, but sometimes people in the pew aren't as excited as they should be. Keep on going, seeing, speaking. If you're faithfully sharing Jesus, you're serving in a growing church.

Success as a ministry wife looks an awful lot like hard work. And fun. When we serve at God's calling and do it with passion, this sixth simple step is not work. It's ministry. And it's a joy.

"He carries you—you carry others. He strengthens you—you strengthen others. He loves you—you love others. He won't stop—you won't either!"
—JEAN FORSYTHE (MRS. RANDY), PORTAGE, IN

NEXT STEP
TAKE ACTION
A LOOK AT THE BOOK
SIMPLE FRESH IDEAS **MY COMMITMENT TO GOD**

❑ I will joyfully say yes every time God prompts me.

❑ I will confidently and kindly say no when God says no.

❑ I will find at least one area of ministry in my church, and work hard to become an expert on it.

❑ I will do every ministry for God with great passion.

❑ I will study God's Word to determine my spiritual gifts.

❑ I will invite one person to my church every week and calendar their name.

NEXT STEP
TAKE ACTION
A LOOK AT THE BOOK
SIMPLE FRESH IDEAS

Pick a couple of these action activities to reinforce your study about serving God.

❑ Make a list of every person you know who may not know Christ personally. Begin with relatives, friends, acquaintances. Include neighbors, doctors, favorite waitress, hair stylist, etc. Begin a new habit of praying for their salvation regularly.

❑ Do a personal Bible study of 1 Peter 4:10–11, 1 Corinthians 12, Ephesians 4, and Romans 12 about spiritual gifts.

❑ Make a list of your spiritual gifts and talents on one side of a paper. Make a list of the ministries you're involved in at church on the other side. Draw lines between the columns to show how those may intersect.

❑ Help your child determine his or her spiritual gifts. There are many good spiritual gifts tests online for children. Help find an age-appropriate way for him or her to use those gifts in the church.

❏ Memory challenge: "Based on the gift each one has received, use it to serve others, as good managers of the varied grace of God" (1 Peter 4:10).

❏ *What's your easiest method of telling someone about Christ? Do it again today.

❏ Make a commitment to invite one unchurched person to church every week. If you use a calendar or calendar app, write the person's name on the Sunday you invited her, even if she doesn't come. Don't miss any Sundays!

❏ Call your denominational offices to find out what upcoming classes or conferences are available pertaining to the ministry where you serve. Do online research and personal interviews with people who do that same type ministry.

❏ Do a Bible word study on *serve*.

❏ Begin a collection of Bible verses to use as you serve. Print them on sticky-back paper and attach inside the back of your Bible for quick reference.

❏ Watch for pretty notecards on sale, and buy some in case God prompts you to write an encouraging note some day.

❏ *Questions to chat about with a ministry wife:
  ◼ How can I add passion to my current ministry in the church?
  ◼ What's your favorite area to serve in the church?
  ◼ What is your spiritual gift(s)?

❏ Talk with your husband to discover his thoughts about your spiritual gifts.

❏ Treat a mature friend, who knows you well, to lunch. Ask her observations about your spiritual gifts.

❏ Make a list of every activity, hobby, or organization you enjoy (include things like PTO, collect antiques, scrapbooking, love tea, walk the school track, golf league, etc.) Now write ways God could use each one for evangelism.

My Career Is a Missions Field

SIMPLE REMINDERS

- Find ministry opportunities in your employment. God has strategically placed you on that assembly line or courthouse bench to show His light. A nurse may have patients facing death. Share His life! A piano teacher, security guard, homemaker, florist, decorator, student, social worker—no matter what type of employment God has given you—it's your outreach assignment.

- Be an excellent employee or employer. Every Christian represents his or her God and His church at the workplace. That might be extra true for the ministry wife. Always be on time to work. Work hard. Do your best possible work, with joy, a great attitude, and enthusiasm.

- Treat your boss, employees, or co-workers with respect.

- Be a nonverbal witness. Let co-workers see a difference in your life that comes from God. What could you appropriately display at your workstation to show you're God's child? A Bible on your desk? A Christian book on your shelf? A Scripture on your screen saver?

- Never exploit church members because of your job. Be especially cautious if your employment involves sales.

- Never steal from your employer. Don't steal minutes (Internet use during office hours), dollars (borrowing staples for your home), or reputation (speaking ill of your employer).

- Live every minute for Jesus. Let your actions, your clothing, your words, and your attitude shine.

- Read the fourth commandment. Remember the Sabbath, to keep it holy. Many jobs ask that you work on Sunday, but you have a higher priority on Sundays. (Of course there are some exceptions.) Negotiate before you accept a job.

- Be an effective water-cooler witness. Be friendly, sincerely caring about coworkers and customers. Learn their spiritual condition.

Speak conversationally about your church and what God has done for you today. Be a bold witness in an appropriate way for your workplace. Invite co-workers to worship, special events, or Bible study. Pray with them in crisis.

■ Ask God's wisdom in juggling employment, family, and ministry.

Six Simple Steps, in Summary

I'm praying that you have caught a new sense of joy and contentment in serving God alongside your minister-husband. We've chatted about these six simple steps toward joy and contentment as a ministry wife. Check the ones you've committed to accomplish:

❑ Just relax and be the best you, you can be.

❑ Simply smile, and have true joy as you live life for Christ

❑ Love God, love your husband, love your co-laborers, and love your missions field. Lavishly.

❑ When referring to your marriage, family, and church, say "we." It's a team effort.

❑ Be resilient when troubles come your way. Remember God's in control.

❑ Serve God with great passion, as if it's the most important thing in your life. It is.

I hope this primer for ministry wives has reenergized your joy and contentment in your very unique role of ministry. I'm praying that God will use you and your husband in ways you've never imagined to spread His gospel.

And while you're serving, remember that you have a fan applauding you and praying for you in Pensacola, Florida.

Live it. Love it. And keep on shining!

Your friend and fellow ministry wife,

Diana Davis

dianadavis.org

Group Study Guide

**AN EIGHT-SESSION GATHERING, OR
OVERNIGHT RETREAT FOR MINISTRY WIVES**

Overview: A gathering of ministry wives meets for eight monthly sessions, or for an overnight retreat. The purpose is to encourage and inspire those church leaders to great joy and contentment, and to enhance friendship among ministry wives.

Participants: Plan for a specific, limited group of ministry wives with a common interest. Some examples:

- Ministry wives of a multistaff church
- Female seminary students and wives of seminary students
- A group of chaplains' wives
- Missionary wives in a specific country or area
- Denominational leaders' wives who live in a specific area
- Pastors' wives of several nearby Christian churches
- A group of minister of youths' wives in a community
- Wives of evangelists in a county area
- A statewide or community-wide retreat or class for ministry wives
- Wives of bivocational pastors in a county area

- Wives of several large churches in a city
- Seminary professors' wives

This list could go on and on. Determine a target group of ministers' wives who have ministry goals in common with one another.

Class size and meeting place. Reserve a lovely, casual meeting room in a church or home. For an overnight retreat event, chose the best location within half hour drive. The group size could be small (3–6), medium (7–20), or large (such as a statewide retreat for ministry wives.) These suggestions are written for small to medium gathering, but could easily be adjusted for a large group.

Meeting dates and time. Possible suggestion: eight sessions, meeting 7:00 to 8:00 p.m. on the second Tuesday each month, September through November, and January through May. For a retreat, begin Friday evening with dinner and dismiss after an early lunch on Saturday. The class sessions should last an hour maximum (shorter for retreat). Begin and end each session exactly on time. Adjust these suggestions to fit needs of your group.

Invite the participants. Invitations should be issued well ahead. Set a registration deadline so preparations can be made. The invitation should explain who is invited, who is hosting, meeting dates, begin and end time for meetings, and registration method. Promise them great fellowship, inspiration, and encouragement.

If invitations are sent by email, consider sending a personal email note as well as an e-invitation or Facebook event page where they can sign up. If printed invitations are sent, explain registration process and deadline. Follow up a week after invitations are sent, with an email or phone call to confirm their registration.

EIGHT-SESSION CLASS PLAN:

Session 1: Introductory class.

Session 2: Chapter 1 "Just Relax"

Session 3: Chapter 2 "Simply Smile"

Session 4: Chapter 3 "Love Lavishly"

Session 5: Chapter 4 "Say 'We'" (we the couple, we the family sections)

Session 6: Chapter 5 "Be Resilient," and completion of "Say 'We'" chapter

Session 7: Chapter 6 "Serve Passionately"

Session 8: Fellowship cookout or restaurant dinner with spouses

ALTERNATIVE PLAN: OVERNIGHT RETREAT

If you're planning a retreat format, adjust these teaching suggestions to fit, adding lots of fun fellowship activities. A few extra tips can be found at NewHopeDigital.com Here's a sample retreat schedule.

Friday evening:

6:00–6:40 p.m.	Opening Session, with introductions, chapter 1, "Just Relax"
6:40–7:30	Dinner, with chapter 2, "Simply Smile," a fun joy assignment and closing speaker
7:30–8:15	Chapter 3, "Love Lavishly"
8:30	Fellowship

Saturday morning:

8:00–9:15 a.m.	Breakfast, with chapter 4, "Say 'We,'" at breakfast tables beginning at 8:45
9:30–10:15	Chapter 5, "Be Resilient," in outdoor setting if possible; assignment breakout
10:15—10:45	Breakout assignment about chapter 5 or 6
10:45—11:30	Chapter 6, "Serve Passionately," in classroom setting
11:45	Fellowship lunch and closing ceremony
12:30 p.m.	Dismiss

Preparation. For each participant, provide an attractive notebook for handouts and notes, a reusable name tag with large readable font, and *Six Simple Steps*. After the first session, they will be asked to read the next chapter in anticipation of the upcoming class. Reading isn't required, but may help with discussions. (For a retreat, participants are encouraged to at least skim the book.) Prepare any handouts.

At the entry door each session, there is a sign-in sheet, any handouts, and name tags. See notes below for special needs each session. Work hard to create an inviting, joyful atmosphere as they enter.

Room arrangement. For a small group, arrange seating in a circle. A living room setting will work, if you prefer. For a group of ten or more, meet in a classroom, but rearrange the seating for each session—circles, rows, change chair direction, groups of three, etc.

Speakers. The leader will host the group, doing intros, the teaching time, directing group discussion, and closing prayer. She will prepare a teaching time, summarizing what she learned and pointing the class to God's Word on the week's topic. She will preassign a different participant to share the "Storytime" each session—a personal, true story that fits the topic and encourages the listeners. Watch your time!

Planning sheet:

Session	Date	Chapter Topic	Story Time (10 minute speaker)	Refreshments
1		Intro	None	
2		Just Relax		
3		Simply Smile		
4		Say We (We the couple and We the Family sections)		
5		Say We (We the Church section) + Be Resilient		
6		Love Lavishly		
7		Serve Passionately		

Refreshments. Snacks, or at least drinks, help make the evening feel more conducive to fellowship. I'd suggest that the intro session has some really nice snack, such as fresh fruit fondue or veggies and great dips, along with a refreshing ginger ale with cherry juice and maraschino cherry garnish. For sessions 2–7, how about serving only drinks, but really nice ones. For example, during cool months, have a hot chocolate bar with lots of toppings, or several fancy coffees. For warm months, recruit a friend to prepare real fruit smoothies so they're ready to serve at the appropriate time. Session 8 requires no refreshments since it's a dinner.

Group Discussion Questions. Each session, the leader will facilitate a lively, positive sharing time. She may ask if anyone tried a "Take Action" item and discuss. She could come up with a few intriguing discussion questions or use questions under headings marked with an asterisk (*) on that chapter's "Take Action" page. She encourages everyone to participate, and keeps the discussion moving and very positive. If one question bombs, she just moves to the next one. She encourages idea sharing. Remember, this is not a tell-all, whiney class! Keep discussion God honoring. If the group is larger than seven, divide into multiple groups for discussion questions. This should be a highlight of each session!

Prayer Partners and Closing Prayer. At the end of sessions 2–7, ladies will quickly select a new prayer partner, according to the instructions. They sit together, spend a minute chatting, then pray for one another. Some prayer partners may want to communicate by email or meet for coffee during the month—no pressure, though! The leader voices a closing prayer so class ends right on time or early. Refreshments are served afterward.

SESSION 1—INTRODUCTORY FELLOWSHIP

Preparation: Provide a nice notebook with schedule and printed details, a *Six Simple Steps* book, and a participant list with email and phone numbers (with their permission, as checked on their registration form). Print any additional handouts for first chapter. If you want a focal point, bring a pretty fishbowl with a fish in it.

Today's program is primarily for fellowship and introductions. Suggested format:

- **15 minutes**—Refreshments and stand-up mingling as ladies arrive. Music is playing; energy is high. Be friendly and help ladies meet one another.
- **5 minutes**—Welcome and overview—leader. Talk about goals and plans.
- **10 minutes**—Everyone selects their first prayer partner—someone who doesn't look much like you. They sit together for a few minutes, "interviewing" one another so they can introduce to the group. There's a prize for the most interesting or unique introduction! If your group is smaller than four, do this as a whole group.
- **20 minutes**—Introductions. Each person introduces her new prayer partner to the group, giving basic information and interesting tidbits. Award a cute prize to the person and her prayer partner who gave the most interesting introduction.
- **10 minutes**—Closing—the leader may share a Scripture or brief personal story, then prayer partners pray briefly for one another, and leader closes the group time in prayer. Dismiss right on time, or early.

SESSION 2—"JUST RELAX."
Bring lots of decorative pillows to create the Just Relax theme. Provide a few pairs of clean house slippers at the door for those who want them. Prepare any special handouts.

Schedule for Sessions 2–7

5 minutes	Welcome and intros—leader or assigned person
15 minutes	"Teaching time"—leader
10 minutes	"Storytime" testimony

20 minutes   Group discussion, prompted by leader

10 minutes   Choose prayer partners; prayer; closing remarks

Prayer partners: This session, ladies select a new prayer partner whose smile is similar to their own. They spend the last 10 minutes of class meeting one another and praying for each other. The leader closes the group in prayer, right on time.

SESSION 3—"SIMPLY SMILE"

■ Glue paper frowns and sad mouths and smiles to tongue depressors. (Purchase, or make with downloadable art on Google or Pinterest. Print on thick paper and attach to sticks.) Take a group photo with frowns, then smiles. For next session, enlarge the photos for the wall or show on PowerPoint.

■ If you'd like, bring pages of smiley face stickers as handouts.

■ Send an email this week asking participants to email you a snapshot of themselves with their husband, their family, and a photo of their church or worship center. Arrange assistance for digital photos if someone needs it. These will be used in "Say 'We'" session.

■ It would be good for the leader to call participants to ask how they're enjoying class. If someone happens to tell you their kids did the poem rap from this session's "Take Action" sheet, ask them to bring a homemade digital video and show it to class!

SESSION 4—"LOVE LAVISHLY"

■ Hang four large stick-on tear sheets or poster boards on different walls. Label them: *Love God, Love my husband, Love my co-laborers, Love my missions field*. Provide several markers for each.

■ As they arrive, ask everyone to write an idea on at least one sheet (i.e., a way I show love to my ministry co-laborers, etc.)

- Ask today, and send an email reminder, for participants to email their three photos you requested—couple, family, church. We'll use these next session.
- For group discussion, you could ask ladies to share ideas and write them on tear sheets now instead of intro activity.
- For prayer partners, ladies select someone with children or grandchildren of similar ages.

SESSION 5—"SAY WE"

- Use submitted photos to create a looped slide show or PowerPoint to play during class today.
- Bring M&M's, and put them in a bowl or two. Designate someone to hold the M&M's and give them a plastic glove to wear. During group discussion, convince the group that the Ms are really Ws (for "We"). During the discussion questions, each time someone uses a "we"-type pronoun (*us*, *our*, etc.), they'll receive a W&W's candy piece. If it becomes too interruptive, just laugh and pass the bowl of W&W's candies around the circle to share.
- For prayer partners, put the same number of M&M's as your attendance, with two of each color, or multiples of two. Each person takes a candy and finds a prayer partner with matching color.

SESSION 6—"BE RESILIENT"

- Print handout, including printed details about session 8's dinner with husbands. Find an online spiritual gifts test that you like, and include that with handouts.
- You will meet in a different classroom. Post a large arrow sign on the classroom door with note that meeting room has been changed. Several large arrows on walls lead the ministry wives inconveniently through several hallways to meet in a different classroom. Begin the class by talking about resilience when things don't go as planned, like

the lost classroom. Ask a class member with a good camera to bring a tripod and take a fun posed group photo during class.

■ Leader, if you have time, you could send an encouragement note to each class member before this session.

■ For prayer partners, ladies to select someone who serves in a similar church ministry as they do.

SESSION 7—"SERVE PASSIONATELY"

■ Provide another printed invitation with details about the dinner with spouses next session.

■ Overdo a demonstration of lethargy as ladies arrive. You've been friendly and energetic other sessions, but today, act bored and uncaring as they arrive. Yawn. Cross your arms. Look at the ceiling. Send a text when someone's talking to you. You could get another leader in on this with you. During teaching time, ask if anyone noticed the difference in your actions. What a difference passion for serving can make!

■ For prayer partners, ladies select someone with the same number of ears as themselves. (Just pick anyone.)

SESSION 8—DINNER OR COOKOUT WITH SPOUSES

Whether you plan a couples' dinner at a restaurant or family barbecue in a backyard, make this easy and fun. Print the group photo you took and put them in inexpensive frames as a party favor. Prepare name tags with large, readable font for each person. Relax and enjoy great fellowship.